Baby Crochet

Baby Crochet

20 Hand-Crochet Designs for Babies Newborn-24 months

Sandy Powers

Photography by Tara Renaud

SELLERS
PUBLISHING

Published by Sellers Publishing, Inc.
161 John Roberts Road, South Portland, Maine 04106

Visit our Web site: www.sellerspublishing.com
E-mail: rsp@rsvp.com

Design and layout copyright © 2012 BlueRed Press Ltd
Text copyright © 2012 Sandy Powers
Patterns and templates copyright © 2012 Sandy Powers
Photography by Tara Renaud
All rights reserved.
Design by Matt Windsor

ISBN 13: 978-1-4162-0846-4
Library of Congress Number 2012931314

10 9 8 7 6 5 4 3 2

Printed and Bound in China

Contents

Difficulty Key

= Easy

= Intermediate

= Advanced

Crochet Hook Sizes		
METRIC SIZES(mm)	US SIZES	UK/ CANADIAN
2.0	-	14
2.25	B/1	13
2.5	-	12
2.75	C/2	-
3.0	-	11
3.25	D/3	10
3.5	E/4	9
3.75	F/5	-
4.0	G/6	8
4.5	7	7
5.0	H/8	6
5.5	I/9	5
6.0	J/10	4
6.5	K/10 1/2	3
7.0	-	2
8.0	L/11	0
9.0	M/13	00
10.0	N/15	000

Introduction

I first learned to crochet one afternoon after my sister came home from school; she taught me the basics and the rest is, as they say, history. I loved crocheting so much I decided to take a night class at my local high school to learn more about this wonderful craft. I then decided to use my new-found skills and crochet my own designs, little did I know that this would be the first step on the way to becoming a crochet creator and designer. Having had my own family and being a stay-at-home mom, I have been lucky enough to be able to combine my passion for crochet with running a busy household and raising my three children.

I started selling my hand-crafted pieces on the Internet and very quickly realized that there was a real demand for original crochet patterns, so once again my career changed path and I became a pattern creator as well as creating actual pieces. It was very exciting to be approached to create a new book featuring 20 of my favorite new designs. I really enjoyed creating these patterns, combining new ideas and color ways.

I want to thank my daughter, Christina, for all of her help in the making of this book. I want to thank my husband, Jim, for getting us a lot of take-out food while we worked on this book. Also, thank you once again to all of the moms and dads who allowed us to photograph their gorgeous babies and toddlers; it was a lot of fun. The saying 'never work with children or animals' is so true but the results were definitely worth it. I hope you enjoy crocheting these designs for your loved ones as much as I have enjoyed creating them.

Sandy Powers

Hats

Party Hat

This party hat is super fun and easy to make and wear! Made with complementing shades of blue, this hat is sure to be a hit wherever you go.

Materials

- Red Heart Super Saver 7oz/198g/364yds/333m #4 medium weight 100% acrylic
  - Color number 0385 / Color name Royal / 1 skein
  - Color number 0381 / Color name Lt. Blue / 1 skein
  - Color number 0347 / Color name Lt. Periwinkle / 1 skein
- Yarn needle
- Scissors

- **Hook:** US H8/5.00mm

Gauge:
H hook = 4" x 4", 12sc x 12sc rows

Skill level: Intermediate

Glossary of abbreviations

ch – chain
fpsc – front post single crochet
rep – repeat
rnd(s) – round(s)
sc – single crochet
slst – slip stitch
tog – together
yo – yarn over hook

NOTE: to make a fpsc – front post single crochet – insert hook behind sc, and come back up on other side of same single crochet. Yo, drop off 2 loops on hook.

0-3 months = 12" circumference, 4 ¾" tall (please note that '0' months refers to newborns)
3-6 months = 14" circumference, 5" tall
6-12 months = 16" circumference, 5 ½" tall
18-24 months = 18" circumference 6" tall

HAT

For all sizes: follow rnds 1–9 and the strands.

Knob on top of hat

Rnd 1: With H hook and Royal, ch2, 6sc in second ch from hook. Use a placemarker if desired. (6sc)
Rnd 2: 2sc in each sc around. (12sc)
Rnds 3–4: 1sc in each sc around. (12sc)
Rnd 5: (Sc tog the next 2sc) rep 5 more times. (6sc)

STRANDS

1st strand: Slst into next sc, ch25, 1slst in second ch from hook, 1slst in each of the next 23ch, slst same sc.
second strand to 6th strand: 1sc in next sc, ch25, 1slst in second ch from hook, 1slst in each of the next 23ch, slst same sc. At end of 6th strand do not fasten off, continue onto hat again.
Rnd 6: 2sc in each sc from rnd 5, flipping strands towards you and working in between the strands to make 12sc. (12sc) Fasten off Royal. Slst to join.
Rnd 7: With H hook and Lt Blue, attach yarn to where you fastened off. 2sc in same st as joining, 2sc in each sc around. (24sc)
Rnd 8: *1sc in next sc, 2sc in next sc* rep from * to * around. (36sc)
Rnd 9: *1sc in each of the next 2sc, 2sc in next sc* rep from * to * around. (48sc)

0-3 MONTHS SIZE ONLY 14.5"

Rnds 10–14: 1sc in each sc around. (48sc)
Rnd 15: 1fpsc around each sc on rnd 14. Slst to join. Ch1. (48fpsc)
Rnd 16: 1sc in the back of the same st as joining, 1sc in the back of each of the fpsc from rnd 15. Slst to join. Ch1. (48sc)
Rnd 17: 1sc in the same st as joining, 1sc in each of the next 2sc, *sc tog the next 2sc, 1sc in each of the next 3sc*, rep from * to * around. Slst to join. Ch1 (39sc)
Rnds 18–19: 1sc in same st as joining, 1sc in each sc around. Slst to join. Ch1. (39sc)

Sc between the strands.

Showing what fpsc looks like.

Rnd 20: 1fpsc in around same st as joining, 1fpsc around each sc. Slst to join. Fasten off and weave in ends.

3-6 MONTHS SIZE ONLY 15.5"

Rnd 10: *1sc in next 7sc, 2sc in next sc * rep from * to * around. (54sc)

Rnds 11–17: 1sc in each sc around. (54sc)

Rnd 18: 1fpsc around each sc on rnd 17. Slst to join. Ch1. (54fpsc)

Rnd 19: 1sc in the back of the same st as joining, 1sc in the back of each of the fpsc from rnd 18. Slst to join. Ch1. (54sc)

Rnd 20: 1sc in the same st as joining, 1sc in each of the next 3sc, sc tog the next 2sc, *1sc in next 4sc, sc tog the next 2sc * rep from * to * around. Slst to join. Ch1. (45sc)

Rnds 21–22: 1sc in same st as joining, 1sc in each sc around. Slst to join. Ch1. (45sc)

Rnd 23: 1fpsc in around same st as joining, 1fpsc around each sc. Slst to join. Fasten off and weave in ends.

6-12 MONTHS SIZE ONLY 16.5"

Rnd 10: *1sc in each of the next 3sc, 2sc in next sc* rep from * to * around. (60sc)

Rnds 11–20: 1sc in each sc around. (60sc)

Rnd 21: 1fpsc around each sc on rnd 20. Slst to join. Ch 1. (60fpsc)

Rnd 22: 1sc in the back of the same st as joining, 1sc in the back of each of the fpsc from rnd 21. Slst to join. Ch1. (60sc)

Rnd 23: 1sc in the same st as joining, 1sc in each of the next 3sc, sc tog the next 2sc, *1sc in each of the next 4sc, sc tog the next 2sc* rep from * to * around, ending with 1sc in last 5sc. Slst to join. Ch1. (50sc)

Rnds 24–25: 1sc in same st as joining, 1sc in each sc around. Slst to join. Ch1. (50sc)

Rnd 26: 1fpsc in around same st as joining, 1fpsc around each sc. Slst to join. Fasten off and weave in ends.

18 MONTHS TO 24 MONTHS SIZE ONLY

Rnd 10: *1sc in each of the next 3sc, 2sc in next sc* rep from * to * around. (60sc)

Rnd 11: *1sc in each of the next 9sc, 2sc in next sc* rep from * to * around. (66sc)

Rnds 12–23: 1sc in each sc around. (66sc)

Rnd 24: 1fpsc around each sc on rnd 23. Slst to join. Ch1. (66fpsc)

Rnd 25: 1sc in the back of the same st as joining, 1sc in the back of each of the fpsc from rnd 24. Slst to join. Ch1. (66sc)

Rnd 26: 1sc in the same st as joining, 1sc in each of the next 2sc, sc tog the next 2sc, *1sc in each of the next 3sc, sc tog the next 2sc* rep from * to * around. Ending with 1sc in last sc. Slst to join. Ch1. (53sc)

Rnds 27–28: 1sc in same st as joining, 1sc in each sc around. Slst to join. Ch1. (53sc)

Rnd 29: 1fpsc in around same st as joining, 1fpsc around each sc. Slst to join. Fasten off and weave in ends.

DOTS

Make 4 Royal color dots for 0–6 months size; make 5 dots for 6–24 months size.

Make 4 Lt Periwinkle color dots for 0–6 months size; make 5 dots for 6–24 months size.

Rnd 1: With H hook and Royal or Lt Periwinkle, ch2, 6sc in second ch from hook. (6sc)

Rnd 2: (slst, ch1) in each sc around. Slst to join. Fasten off leaving a tail to sew with. Sew dots evenly spaced around on rnds in between the fpsc rnds.

Showing what working behind the fpsc looks like.

Sewing the dots on.

Newsboy Hat

This adorable hat can be worn by boys or girls. Add a cute little flower if desired. Made with berry stitches and front post double crochet.

Materials

- Red Heart Alpaca Love Stitch Nation by Debbie Stoller
  3oz/85g/132yds/121m #4 medium weight
  80% wool/ 20% Alpaca
  – Color number 3520 / color name Peacock Feather / 1 skein
  – Color number 3620 / color name Fern / 1 skein
  – Color number 3810 / color name Lake / small amount for optional flower
- Yarn needle
- 2 x 1/4" leather-look buttons
- Scissors
- Barrette for flower

- **Hooks:** US H (8/5.00mm) and US I (9/5.50mm)

Skill level: Advanced

Gauge:
I hook = 4" x 4"
12sc x 13sc rows

Glossary of abbreviations

BS – berry stitch – insert hook into next sc, bring yarn back thru, (yo, drop off first loop only) rep 2 more times, yo, drop off last 2 loops. Push loops forward to form berry.

ch – chain

dc – double crochet

fpdc – front post double crochet – yo, insert hook behind dc or fpdc, yo, bring yarn back thru, yo, drop off first 2 loops, yo, drop off last 2 loops.

rep – repeat

rnd(s) – round(s)

RS – right side of work

sc – single crochet

sk – skip

slst – slip stitch

WS – wrong side of work

NOTE: follow rnds 1–11 for all sizes, then continue with the instructions for the size you want to make.
Use H hook to make size 6–12 months size hats
Use I hook to make 0–3 months, 3–6 months, 18–24 months size hats
Button band instructions are written first for 0–3 months and other sizes are in parenthesis

0–3 months = 14" circumference, 5" tall
3–6 months = 16" circumference, 5 ½" tall
6–18 months = 18" circumference, 6" tall
18–24 months =18" circumference, 6 ½" tall

HAT

Rnd 1: (RS) With H or I hook and Peacock Feather, ch2, 6sc in second ch from hook. Slst to join. (6sc)

Rnd 2: (RS) Ch1, 2sc in same st as joining, 2sc in each sc around. Slst to join. (12sc)

Rnd 3: (RS) Ch1, 1sc in same st as joining, 1sc in each sc around. Slst to join. (12sc)

Rnd 4: (RS) Ch1, (sc tog the next 2sc) rep 5 more times. Slst to join. (6sc)

Rnd 5: (RS) Ch1, 2sc in same st as joining,2sc in each sc around. Slst to join.(12sc)

Rnd 6: (RS) Ch1, 2sc in same st as joining, 1sc in next sc, 2dc in next sc, *2sc in next sc, 1sc in next sc, 2dc in next sc* rep from * to* 2 more times. Slst to join. Turn. (20sts)

Rnd 7: (WS) Ch1, 1sc in same st as joining, 1sc in each sc around. Slst to join. Turn. (20sc)

Rnd 8: (RS) Ch1, 2sc in same st as joining, BS in next sc, 2sc in next sc, 1fpdc around each of the next 2dc, *2sc in next sc, BS in next sc, 2sc in next sc, 1fpdc around each of the next 2dc* rep 2 more times. Slst to join. Turn. (28sts)

Rnd 9: (WS) Ch1, 1sc in same st as

Fpdc around dc.

Berry Stitch. Drop off first loop 3.

joining, 1sc in each sc around. Slst to join. Turn. (28sc)

Rnd 10: (RS) Ch1, 2sc in same st as joining, BS in next sc, 1sc in next sc, BS in next sc, 2sc in next sc, 1fpdc around each of the next 2fpdc, *2sc in next sc, BS, 1sc in next sc, BS, 2sc in next sc, 1fpdc around each of the next 2fpdc* rep from * to * 2 more times. Slst to join. Turn. (36sts)

Rnd 11: (WS) Ch1, 1sc in same st as joining, 1sc in each sc around. Turn. (36sc)

0-3 MONTHS SIZE ONLY

Use I hook.

Rnd 12: (RS) Ch1, 1sc in same st as joining, BS, 1sc, BS, 1sc, BS, 1sc, 1fpdc around each of the next 2fpdc, *1sc, BS, 1sc, BS, 1sc, BS, 1sc, 1fpdc around each of the next 2fpdc* rep from * to * 2 more times. Turn. (36sts)

Rnds 13–20: Repeat rnds 11 and 12 alternately. Do not turn at end of rnd 20. Continue on to brim of hat.

3–6 MONTHS SIZE ONLY

Use I hook.

Rnd 12: (RS) Ch1, 2sc in same st as joining, BS, 1sc, BS, 1sc, BS, 2sc, 1fpdc around each of the next 2fpdc, *2sc, BS, 1sc, BS, 1sc, BS, 2sc, 1fpdc around each of the next 2fpdc* rep from * to * 2 more times. Turn. (44sts)

Rnd 13: (WS) Ch1, 1sc in same st as joining, 1sc in each sc around. Turn. (44sc)

Rnd 14: (RS) Ch1, 1sc in same st as joining, BS, 1sc, BS, 1sc, BS, 1sc, 1fpdc around each of the next 2fpdc, *1sc, BS, 1sc, BS, 1sc, BS, 1sc, 1fpdc around each of the next 2fpdc* rep from * to * 2 more times. Turn. (44sts)

Rnds 15–22: Repeat rnds 13 and 14 alternately. At end of rnd 22 do not turn. Continue on to instructions for brim.

18 MONTHS TO 24 MONTHS SIZE ONLY

Use I hook.

Rnd 12: (RS) Ch1, 2sc in same st as joining, BS, 1sc, BS, 1sc, BS, 2sc, 1fpdc around each of the next 2fpdc, *2sc, BS, 1sc, BS, 1sc, BS, 2sc, 1fpdc around each of the next 2fpdc * rep from * to * 2 more times. Turn. (44sts)

Rnd 13: (WS) Ch1, 1sc in same st as joining, 1sc in each sc around. Turn. (44sc)

Rnd 14: (RS) Ch1, 2sc in same st as joining, BS, 1sc, BS, 1sc, BS, 1sc, BS, 2sc, 1fpdc around each of the next 2fpdc, *2sc, BS, 1sc, BS, 1sc, BS, 1sc, BS, 2sc, 1fpdc around each of the next 2fpdc * rep from * to * 2 more times. Turn. (52sts)

Rnd 15: (WS) Ch1, 1sc in same st as joining, 1sc in each sc around. Turn. (52sc)

Rnd 16: (RS) Ch1, 1sc in same st as joining, BS, 1sc, BS, 1sc, BS, 1sc, BS, 1sc, 1fpdc around each of the next 2fpdc, *1sc, BS, 1sc, BS, 1sc, BS, 1sc, BS, 1sc, BS, 1sc, 1fpdc around each of the next 2fpdc * rep from * to * 2 more times. Turn. (52sts)

Rnds 17–26: Repeat rnds 15 and 16 alternately. At end of rnd 26 do not turn. Continue onto instructions for brim.

BRIM FOR ALL SIZES

Row 1: 2sc in backloop of same st as joining, 2sc in backloops of next 6sts (8sts, 10sts, 10sts). Turn. (14sc, 18sc, 22sc, 22sc)

Row 2: Ch1, sk first sc, 1sc in next 11sc (14sc, 19sc, 19sc) sk next sc, 1sc in next sc. Turn. (12sc, 16sc, 20sc, 20sc)

Row 3: Ch1, sk first sc, 1sc in next 9sc (13sc, 17sc, 17sc) sk next sc, 1sc in next sc. (10sc, 14sc, 18sc, 18sc) do not turn.

Next: Slst in ends of rows down left side of brim back to bottom of hat. 1sc in next 29sts, (34sts, 40sts, 40sts) slst in next st, 1sc in ends of rows on brim of hat, sk next sc, 1sc in next 7sc, (11sc, 15sc, 15sc) sk next sc, 1sc in next sc, 1sc in ends of rows down left side of brim, slst in next 2sts. Fasten off and weave in ends. Follow instructions for button band for this size.

Then drop off last 2 loops to complete berry stitch. Push ch forward.

Sc in the backloops for start of brim.

Sc in each end of row on brim.

BUTTON BANDS FOR ALL SIZES

Rnd 1: With H hook and Fern, ch22, (ch24, ch26, ch28), 4sc in second ch from hook, 1sc in next 19ch (21ch, 23ch, 25ch), 8sc in last ch. Now working on opposite side of ch, 1sc in next 19ch (21ch, 23ch, 25ch) 4sc in same ch as beg. Slst to first sc to join. Fasten off leaving a tail to sew with. Sew buttons to each end. Sew band onto front of hat.

OPTIONAL FLOWER

Rnd 1: With H hook and Lake, ch2, 6sc in second ch from hook. Slst to join. (6sc)

Petals

Ch3, 2dc in same st as joining, ch3, slst in same st, (slst, ch3, 2dc, ch3, slst all in next sc) rep 4 more times to make 6 petals all together. Fasten off leaving a tail to sew with.

Center Dot

Rnd 1: With H hook and Fern, ch2, 5sc in second ch from hook. Slst to join. (5sc)
Rnds 2–3: Ch1, 1sc in same st as joining, 1sc in each sc around. Slst to join. (5sc) End or rnd3, fasten off leaving a tail to sew with. Sew center dot to center of flower. Sew flower onto barrette.

Sk sc and work sc in next sc.

Work 8sc in end of row. Sc in opposite side of ch for button band.

Curly Cue Hat

Let your little one show off their fun and unique personality with this adorable curly cue hat! The adorable curls are sure to bring a smile to everyone's face.

Materials

- Red Heart Super Saver 7oz/198g/364yds/333m #4 medium weight 100% acrylic
- Color number 0724 / color name Baby Pink / 1 skein
- Bernat Softee Baby 5oz/140g/362yds/331m #3 light weight 100% acrylic
- Color number 30205 / color name Prettiest Pink / 1 skein
- Yarn needle
- Scissors

- **Hook:** US H (8/5.00mm)

Skill level: Easy

Gauge:
H hook = 4" x 4"
12½sc x 13sc rows

Glossary of abbreviations

ch – chain
dc – double crochet
rnd(s) – round(s)
sc – single crochet
slst – slip stitch

NOTE: instructions written for 0-3 months; other sizes are in parenthesis

0-3 months = 14"
3-6 months = 15"
6-12 months = 16"
18-24 months = 17"

HAT

Rnd 1: With Baby Pink and H hook ch19 (ch21, ch24, ch27), 2sc in second ch from hook, 1sc in each of the next 16ch (18ch, 21ch, 24ch), 4sc in last ch. Now working on opposite side of ch, 1sc in each of the next 16ch (18ch, 21ch, 24ch), 2sc in same st as beg. Continue going around using a place marker. (40sc, 44sc, 50sc, 56sc)
Rnd 2: 1sc in each sc around. (40sc, 44sc, 50sc, 56sc)
Repeat rnd 2 until hat measures 4" (4.5", 5", 5.5"s) tall.

FIRST EARFLAP

Row 1: 1sc in next 8sc. Ch1, turn, leaving the rest of the rnd unworked for now.
Rows 2–3: 1sc in next 8sc. Ch1, turn. (8sc)
Row 4: Sc tog the first 2sc, 1sc in next 4sc, sc tog the last 2sc. Ch1, turn. (6sc)
Row 5: 1sc in next 6sc. Ch1, turn. (6sc)
Row 6: Sc tog the first 2sc, 1sc in next 2sc, sc tog the last 2sc. Ch1, turn. (4sc)
Row 7: 1sc in next 4sc. Ch1, turn. (4sc)
Row 8: (Sc tog the next 2sc) repeat one more time. Ch1, turn. (2sc)
Row 9: 1sc in next 2sc. Do not turn.

Ch1. (2sc)
Next: 1slst in each end of row down left side of earflap, 1sc in next 20sc (22sc, 25sc, 28sc). Ch1, turn.

SECOND EARFLAP

Row 1: 1sc in next 8sc. Ch1, turn. (8sc)
Row 2: 1sc in next 8sc. Ch1, turn. (8sc)
Row 3: Sc tog the first 2sc, 1sc in next 4sc, sc tog the last 2sc. Ch1, turn. (6sc)
Row 4: 1sc in next 6sc. Ch1, turn. (6sc)
Row 5: Sc tog the first 2sc, 1sc in next 2sc, sc tog the last 2sc. Ch1, turn. (4sc)
Row 6: 1sc in next 4sc. Ch1, turn. (4sc)
Row 7: (Sc tog the next 2sc) repeat

one more time. Ch1, turn. (2sc)

Row 8: 1sc in next 2sc. Do not turn. Ch1. (2sc)

Next: 1slst in each end of row down left side of earflap, 1sc in next 12sc (14sc, 17sc, 20sc). Do not fasten off but continue on to trim.

TRIM

Rnd 1: 1sc in each end of row on each earflap and 1sc in each sc around. Slst to join. Fasten off and weave in ends.

Rnd 2: With H hook and Prettiest Pink, attach yarn to where you fastened off. 1sc in same st as joining, 1sc in each sc to first tip of earflap, (first tie) ch31, 1slst in second ch from hook, 1slst in each rem ch, 1sc in each sc to second tip of earflap, (second tie) ch31, 1slst in second ch from hook, 1slst in each rem ch, 1sc in each sc to end of rnd. Slst to join. Fasten off and weave in ends.

Ch31, 1slst in 2nd ch from hook, 1slst in each rem ch to make 1st tie.

Attach to top of hat to start curls.

Above and top right: 2sc in each ch to make curls.

CURLS

NOTE: work same for each side of hat.

1st curl: With H hook and Prettiest Pink, attach yarn to corner of hat, ch20, 2sc in second ch from hook, 1sc in each rem ch, slst into same beg st.

2nd curl: Ch35, 2sc in second ch from hook, 2sc in each rem ch, slst into same beg st.

3rd curl: Ch25, 2sc in second ch from hook, 2sc in each rem ch. Slst into same beg st. fasten off and weave in ends.

Shamrock Head Cover

This cute hat with little shamrocks hanging down the sides can bring the luck of the Irish to any baby! Made with soft DK weight cotton, this hat is fun and easy to make.

Materials

- Dale of Norway Piper Cotton Yarn 1.75oz/50g/114yds/105m
  – Color number 75772 / Color name Tide / 1 skein
  – Color number 75771 / Color name Palm / 1 skein
  or any DK weight yarns
- Yarn needle
- Scissors

- **Hook:** US G (6/4.00mm)

Gauge:
G hook = 4" x 4", 12sc x 12sc rows

Skill level: Easy

Glossary of abbreviations

beg – beginning
ch – chain
dc – double crochet
hdc – half double crochet
rnd(s) – round(s)
sc – single crochet
slst – slip stitch

NOTE: instructions written first for 0–3 months, the rest are in parenthesis

0-3 months = 14"
3-6 months = 15"
6-12 months = 16"
18-24 months = 17"

HAT

Rnd 1: With Tide and G hook ch 21(ch23, ch26, ch29), 2sc in second ch from hook, 1sc in each of the next 18ch (20ch, 23ch, 26ch), 4sc in last ch. Now working on opposite side of ch, 1sc in each of the next 18ch (20ch, 23ch, 26ch), 2sc in same st as beg. Slst to join. (44sc, 48sc, 54sc, 60sc)
Rnd 2: Ch1, 1sc in same st as joining, 1sc in each sc around. Slst to join. Ch1. repeat rnd 2 until hat measures 4" (4.5", 5", 5.5"). Continue on to instructions for cuff.

Cuff

Row 1: Ch4, 1sc in second ch from hook, 1sc in each of the next 3ch, 1slst in same beg st, 1slst in next 2sc. Turn. (3sc)
Row 2: Ch1, skip next 3slst, 1sc in the backloop of next 3sc. Turn.
Row 3: Ch1, 1sc in the backloop of next 3sc, 1slst in same beg st, 1slst in next 2sc. Turn. (3sc)
Row 4: Ch1, skip the first 3slst, 1sc in the backloop of each of the next 3sc. Turn.
Rows 5–40 (5–48, 5–54, 5–60): Repeat rows 3 and 4 alternately. Fasten off at end of last row. Sew row 1 to row 40 (48, 54, 60) to close cuff. Weave in ends.

SHAMROCKS

1st shamrock: With Palm and G hook, attach yarn to corner of hat, ch11, 1hdc in 3rd ch from hook, 3dc in same ch, 1hdc in same ch, 1sc in same ch, 1slst in next ch, (1slst, 1sc, 1hdc,

Working on opposite side of ch.

Working in back loop.

Chain for shamrock.

3dc, 1hdc, 1sc, 1slst) all in next ch, 1slst in next ch, (1slst, 1sc, 1hdc, 3dc, 1hdc, 1sc, 1slst) all in next ch, slst to first petal to join. 1slst in each of the remaining chs, 1slst in corner of hat. Ch18.

2nd shamrock: 1hdc in 3rd ch from hook, 3dc in same ch, 1hdc in same ch, 1sc in same ch, 1slst in next ch, (1slst, 1sc, 1hdc, 3dc, 1hdc, 1sc, 1slst) all in next ch, 1slst in next ch, (1slst, 1sc, 1hdc, 3dc, 1hdc, 1sc, 1slst) all in next ch, slst in first petal to join, 1slst in each of the remaining chs, 1slst in corner of hat. Ch14.

3rd shamrock: 1hdc in 3rd ch from hook, 3dc in same ch, 1hdc in same ch, 1sc in same ch, 1slst in next ch, (1slst, 1sc, 1hdc, 3dc, 1hdc, 1sc, 1slst) all in next ch, 1slst in next ch, (1slst, 1sc, 1hdc, 3dc, 1hdc, 1sc, 1slst) all in next ch, slst in first petal of shamrock, 1slst in each of the remaining chs, 1slst in corner of hat. Fasten off and weave in ends.

Repeat for other side of hat.

FRONT SHAMROCK

With Palm and G hook, (1st petal) ch3, 1hdc in 3rd ch from hook, 3dc in same ch, 1hdc in same ch, 1sc in same ch, 1slst in same ch, (2nd petal) (ch3, 1hdc, 3dc, 1hdc, 1sc, 1slst all in 3rd ch from hook,) (3rd petal) rep one more time, slst to beg petal to form a shamrock, then ch6, 1slst in second ch from hook, 1slst in next 4ch. Fasten off leaving a tail to sew with. Sew shamrock onto front of hat.

First petal on shamrock.

3rd petal on shamrock.

Join 3rd petal to finish shamrock.

Woodland Long Elf Hat

0-3 months

This adorable hat makes a great photo prop for your little elf! This hat is created using a super soft and fluffy medium weight yarn, and the roses are easy to make and sew onto the hat.

Materials

- Jiffy 3oz/85g/135yds/123m #5 bulky weight 100% acrylic yarns (purchased at AC Moore Craft Store)
- Color number 099 / color name Fisherman / 2 skeins
- Color number 402 / color name Purple Spray / 1 skein
- Color number 138 / color name Grape / 1 skein
- Red Heart Super Saver 7oz/198g/364yds/333m #4 medium weight 100% acrylic
- Color number 0624 / color name Tea Leaf / 1 skein
- Yarn needle
- Scissors

- Hooks: US J (10/6.00mm) and US K (10.5/6.50mm)

Gauge:
K hook = 3" x 3"
8dc x 3dc rows

Skill level: Intermediate

Glossary of abbreviations

ch – chain
dc – double crochet
hdc – half double crochet
picot – dc, ch2 in top of dc
rnd(s) – round(s)
sc – single crochet
slst – slip stitch

Warning – never leave a baby unattended while wearing this hat. This hat was designed for photo prop pictures.

NOTE: work all dc in backloops. Ch1 at beg of each rnd, do not count it as a stitch and work 1dc in the same st as the ch1.

0-3 months = 14" circumference, can be made as short or as long as desired

HAT

Rnd 1: With K hook and Fisherman, ch2, 6sc in 2rd ch from hook. Continue in a spiral fashion, using a placemarker if desired. (6sc)

Rnd 2: 2dc in each sc around. (12dc)

Rnds 3–6: 1dc in each dc around. (12dc)

Rnd 7: 1dc in each dc around and at the same time add one more dc to rnd. (13dc)

Rnds 8–12: 1dc in each dc around. (13dc)

Rnds 13–42: Repeat rnds 7–12 in sequence. At end of rnd 42 you will have 18dc.

Rnd 43: 1dc in each dc around and at the same time add 4 more dc to rnd. (22dc)

Rnd 44: 1dc in each dc around and at the same time add 6 more dc to rnd. (28dc)

Rnd 45: 1dc in each dc around and at the same time add 6 more dc to each rnd. (34dc)

Rnds 46–50: 1dc in each dc around. (34dc)

Rnd 51: Change to a J hook, 1sc in the backloops of each sc around. (34sc)

Rnds 52–60: 1sc in both loops in each sc around. Roll rnds 51 to 60 up as shown in pictures.

Warning – never leave a baby unattended while wearing this hat. This hat was designed for photo prop pictures.

Attach yarn to first unworked loop to make vine.

Slst, ch1 in each unworked loop specified on pattern to create climbing vine.

CLIMBING VINE

With J hook and Tea Leaf, and with opening of hat facing you, attach yarn to first unworked loop, (1slst, ch1) in next 25 unworked loops, *slst into unworked loop in rnd above where you are working, (1slst, ch1) in next 25 unworked loops*. Repeat from * to * 2 more times, then, repeat the same as in * to *, but only work in 15 unworked loops for two times, going up a rnd after every 15 unworked loops are made.

Then repeat same as in * to *, but only work in 10 unworked loops and then go up a rnd after every 10 unworked loops are made. Keep working your way up a rnd after you fill in every 10 unworked loops, and continue to do this until you reach the tip of the hat.

FLOWER

With J hook and Purple Spray, and leaving starting tail about 8" long, ch17, 1dc in 3rd ch from hook, 1dc in next 14ch. Fasten off leaving a long tail to sew with. Roll dc into a ball that will look like a rose. Sew end closed with starting tail and run a stitch thru all the rolls to hold flower together. Fasten off. Use ending tail to sew flower onto hat after you put the leaf on it.
NOTE: you can also alternate the color of the flowers. I added in grape colored flowers on my hat.

LEAF

Rnd 1: With J hook and Tea Leaf, ch2, 5sc in second ch from hook. (5sc)
Rnd 2: 1sc in next sc, (1sc, 1hdc, 1dc, ch2, slst in top of dc to form a picot, 1dc, 1hdc, 1sc) all in next sc, 1sc in next 3sc. Slst in next sc to end. Fasten off leaving a tail to sew with. Sew leaf to back side of flower, leaving some sticking out as shown in pictures.
NOTE: after I put all my flowers on, I rolled my brim up and tack it down so it would stay rolled. Just a suggestion.

Picot stitch to make point of leaf.

Roll stitches to look like a rose.

This is what your rose will look like after you roll it.

Beanie with Sheep Applique

Quick and easy to make, this hat is sure to be a favorite.

Materials

- Bernat Baby Coordinates 5oz/140g/388yds/355m #3 light weight 75.2% acrylic, 22.2% rayon, 2.6% nylon
  - Color number 48128 / color name Soft Blue / 1 skein
  - Color number 48228, color name Iced Mint / 1 skein
- Bernat Soft Boucle 5oz/140g/255yds/233m #5 bulky weight 97%acrylic, 3%polyester
  - Color number 06703 / color name Natural / 1oz for sheep
- Red Heart Super Saver 7oz/198g/364yds/333m #4 medium weight 100% acrylic
  - Color number 0312 / color name Black / 1oz for sheep
- Yarn needle
- Scissors

- **Hooks:** US G (6/4.00mm) and US H (8/5.00mm)

Skill level: Easy

Gauge:
G hook = 4"x 4"
16sc x 16sc rows

Glossary of abbreviations

ch – chain
dc – double crochet
rnd(s) – round(s)
sc – single crochet
slst – slip stitch

NOTE: CH3 counts as first dc
Follow rnds 1-3 for all sizes

0-3 months = 12" circumference, 4¾" tall
3-6 months = 14" circumference, 5" tall
6-12 months = 16" circumference, 5½" tall
18-24 months = 18" circumference 6" tall

BEANIE

Rnd 1: With G hook and Soft Blue, ch3, 11dc in 3rd ch from hook. Slst to join. (12dc)
Rnd 2: Ch3, 1dc in same st as joining, 2dc in each dc around. Slst to join. (24dc)
Rnd 3: Ch3, 2dc in next dc, *1dc in next dc, 2dc in next dc* rep from * to * around. Slst to join. (36dc)

0–3 MONTHS SIZE ONLY

Rnd 4: Ch3, 1dc in next 3dc, 2dc in next dc, *1dc in next 4dc, 2dc in next dc* rep from * to * around. Slst to join. (42dc)
Rnds 5–7: Ch3, 1dc in each dc around. Slst to join. (42dc) At end of rnd 7 fasten off and weave in ends.
Rnd 8: With G hook and Iced Mint, attach yarn to where you fastened off, 1sc in same st as joining, 1sc in each dc around. Slst to join. (42sc)
Rnds 9–12: Ch1, 1sc in same st as joining, 1sc in each sc around. Slst to join. (42sc) At end of rnd 12 fasten off and weave in ends.

3–6 MONTHS SIZE ONLY

Rnd 4: Ch3, 1dc in next dc, 2dc in next dc, *1dc in next 2dc, 2dc in next dc*

Attach Black yarn in any sc to make head.

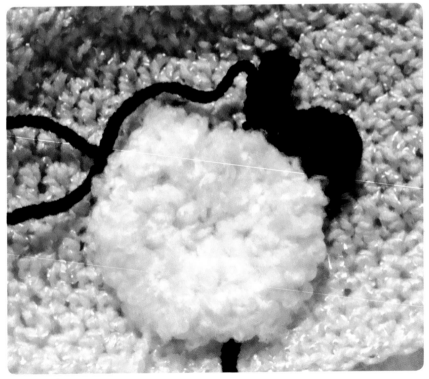

Sew ear down.

rep from * to * around. Slst to join. (48dc)

Rnds 5–8: Ch3, 1dc in each dc around. Slst to join. (48dc) At end of rnd 8 fasten off and weave in ends.

Rnd 9: With G hook and Iced Mint, attach yarn to where you fastened off, 1sc in same st as joining, 1sc in each dc around. Slst to join. (48sc)

Rnds 10–13: Ch1, 1sc in same st as joining, 1sc in each sc around. Slst to join. (48sc) At end of rnd 13 fasten off and weave in ends.

6–12 MONTHS SIZE ONLY

Rnd 4: Ch3, 1dc in next dc, 2dc in next dc, *1dc in next 2dc, 2dc in next dc* rep from * to * around. Slst to join. (48dc)

Rnd 5: Ch3, 1dc in next 6dc, 2dc in next dc, *1dc in next 7dc, 2dc in next dc* rep from * to * around. Slst to join. (54dc)

Rnds 6–9: Ch3, 1dc in each dc around. Slst to join. (54dc) At end of rnd 9 fasten off and weave in ends.

Rnd 10: With G hook and Iced Mint, attach yarn to where you fastened off, 1sc in same st as joining, 1sc in each dc around. Slst to join. (54sc)

Rnds 11–14: Ch1, 1sc in same st as joining, 1sc in each sc around. Slst to join. (54sc) At end of rnd 14 fasten off and weave in ends.

18–24 MONTHS SIZE ONLY

Rnd 4: Ch3, 1dc in next dc, 2dc in next dc, *1dc in next 2dc, 2dc in next dc* rep from * to * around. Slst to join. (48dc)

Rnd 5: Ch3, 1dc in next 2dc, 2dc in next dc, *1dc in next 3dc, 2dc in next dc* rep from * to * around. Slst to join. (60dc)

Rnds 6–11: Ch3, 1dc in each dc around. Slst to join. (60dc) At end of rnd 11 fasten off and weave in ends.

Rnd 12: With G hook and Iced Mint, attach yarn to where you fastened off, 1sc in same st as joining, 1sc in each

dc around. Slst to join. (60sc)
Rnds 13–16: Ch1, 1sc in same st as joining, 1sc in each sc around. Slst to join. (60sc) At end of rnd 16 fasten off and weave in ends.

SHEEP APPLIQUE
Body
Rnd 1: With H hook and Natural, ch2, 6sc in second ch from hook. Continue in a spiral fashion. (6sc)
Rnd 2: 2sc in each sc around. (12sc)
Rnd 3: 2sc in each sc around. (24sc) fasten off and leaving a tail to sew with.

Face and Ear
Turn body to the wrong side of work. With H hook and Black, attach yarn to any sc. (1sc, 1hdc, 1dc, 1hdc, 1sc, 1slst) all in same sc, (ear) ch4, 1slst in second ch from hook, 1slst in next 2ch slst in same sc as beg. Fasten off leaving a tail to sew with. Fold ear over and tack down.

Tail
With H hook and Black, skip next 11sc, attach yarn to next sc, ch3, 1slst in second ch from hook, 1slst in next ch, slst in same sc as beg. Fasten off and weave in ends.

Feet
With H hook and Black, skip next 4sc, attach yarn to next sc, 3sc in same sc, 1slst in next 2sc, 3sc in next sc, slst in same sc. Fasten off leaving a tail to sew with.
Sew sheep to hat with Natural. Then sew the face and feet to hat. Weave in all ends.

Attach tail to opposite side of head.

Attach feet to bottom of circle, weave in all ends.

Body Suits

Baby Bunting

Baby will stay warm and snuggly in this adorable bunting.

Materials

- Cascade Pure Alpaca 3.5oz/100g/220yds/200m #4 medium weight 100% Baby Alpaca
- Color number 3030 / color name Summer Sky Heather / 3 skeins
- Color number 3022 / color name Citron / 1 skein
- Yarn needle
- Scissors
- Velcro strips
- Fabric glue

- Hooks: US F (5/4.00mm) and US G (6/4.50mm)

Skill level: Intermediate

Gauge:
14 pattern rows – 4",
8 pattern sts = 4"

Glossary of abbreviations

beg – beginning
ch – chain
chsp – chain space
corner – (1dc, ch2, 1dc) in chsp
dc – double crochet
hdc – half double crochet
pattern stitch – (1sc, 1hdc) –
   1 single crochet and 1 half
   double crochet in same
   single crochet
rep – repeat
rnd(s) – round(s)
sc – single crochet
sk – skip
slst – slip stitch
st – stitch

Ch2 counts as first dc

0-6 months size measurements = Yoke 16" circumference; body 18" long; sleeves 6" long; hood 8" tall

BUNTING

Yoke

Row 1: With F hook and Summer Sky Heather, ch35, 1dc in 3rd ch from hook, 1dc in next 3ch, (1dc, ch2, 1dc) in next ch, 1dc in next 5ch, (1dc, ch2, 1dc) in next ch, 1dc in next 10ch, (1dc, ch2, 1dc) in next ch, 1dc in next 5ch, (1dc, ch2, 1dc) in next ch, 1dc in next 5ch. Turn. (38dc)

Row 2: Ch2, 1dc in next 5dc, corner in next chsp, 1dc in next 7dc, corner, 1dc in next 12dc, corner, 1dc in next 7dc, corner, 1dc in next 6dc. Turn. (46dc)

Row 3: Ch2, 1dc in next 6dc, corner, 1dc in next 9dc, corner, 1dc in next 14dc, corner, 1dc in next 9dc, corner, 1dc in next 7dc. Turn. (54dc)

Row 4: Ch2, 1dc in next 7dc, corner, 1dc in next 11dc, corner, 1dc in next 16dc, corner, 1dc in next 11dc, corner, 1dc in next 8dc. Turn. (62dc)

Row 5: Ch2, 1dc in next 8dc, corner, 1dc in next 13dc, corner, 1dc in next 18dc, corner, 1dc in next 13dc, corner, 1dc in next 9dc. Turn. (70dc)

Row 6: Ch2, 1dc in next 9dc, corner, 1dc in next 15dc, corner, 1dc in next 20dc, corner, 1dc in next 15dc, corner, 1dc in next 10dc. Turn. (78dc)

Row 7: Ch2, 1dc in next 10dc, corner, 1dc in next 17dc, corner, 1dc in next 22dc, corner, 1dc in next 17dc, corner, 1dc in next 11dc. Turn. (86dc)

Row 8: Ch2, 1dc in next 11dc, corner, 1dc in next 19dc, corner, 1dc in next 24dc, corner, 1dc in next 19dc, corner, 1dc in next 12dc. Turn. (94dc)

Forming arm openings

Row 9: Ch2, 1dc in next 12dc, 1dc in next chsp, ch4, sk next 21dc, 1dc in next chsp, 1dc in next 26dc, 1dc in next chsp, ch4, sk next 21dc, 1dc in next chsp, 1dc in next 13dc. Turn.

Body

Row 10: Change to G hook, ch1, *1sc in next st, 2sc in next st* rep from * to * across row. Turn. (96sc)

Row 11: Ch1, (1sc, 1hdc) in next sc, *sk next sc, (1sc, 1hdc) in next sc* rep from * to * across row ending with 1sc in last sc. Turn.

Row 12: Ch1, (1sc, 1hdc) in first sc, *sk next hdc, (1sc, 1hdc) in next sc* rep from * to * across row ending with 1sc in last sc. Turn.

Repeat row 12 until bunting measures 18" from underarm to bottom of bunting. Fasten off.

HOOD

Row 1: With G hook and Summer Sky Heather, and with right side of neck facing you, count over 3sc from front edge, attach yarn, 1sc in same st as joining, 2sc in each to last 3sc. Turn. (66sc)

Row 2: Ch1, (1sc, 1hdc) in first sc, *sk next sc, (1sc, 1hdc) in next sc* rep from *to * across, ending with 1sc in last st. Turn. (66sts)

Rows 3–23: Ch1, (1sc, 1hdc) in first sc, *sk next hdc, (1sc, 1hdc) in next sc* rep from * to * across, ending with 1sc in last st. Turn. (66sts) At end of row 23 fold hood in half to wrong side and sc the two sides together. Fasten off and weave in ends.

TRIM

Rnd 1: Turn bunting to right side, with Summer Sky Heather and F hook, attach yarn to bottom of bunting, 1sc in same st as joining, 1sc in ends of rows, 1sc in each end of row up to neck edge, 1sc in each end of row around hood opening, 1sc in each end of row back to bottom of bunting. Slst to end rnd. Fasten off and weave in ends.

SLEEVES – MAKE 2

Rnd 1: With G hook and Summer Sky Heather, attach yarn to any st in the underarm hole, 1sc in each st around. Slst to join. Turn. (34sc)

Rnd 2: Ch1, (1sc, 1hdc) in same st as joining, *skip next sc, (1sc, 1hdc) in next sc* rep from * to * around. Slst to join. Turn. (34sts)

Rnds 3–19: Ch1, (1sc, 1hdc) in first sc, *skip next hdc, (1sc, 1hdc) in next sc* rep from * to * around. Slst to join. Turn. (34sts)

Rnd 20: 1sc in same st as joining, *sc tog the next 2sts, 1sc in next st* repeat from * to * around. Slst to join. (23sts) Fasten off, weave in ends.

CUFFS

Rnd 1: With F hook and Citron, attach yarn to where you fastened off. 1sc in same st as joining, 1sc in each st around. Slst to join. Turn. (23sc)

Rnds 2–10: Ch1, 1sc in same st as joining, 1sc in each sc around. Slst

Step 1: Sc together the top of hood, working thru both thicknesses.

to join. Turn. (23sc) At end of rnd 10, fasten off, weave in ends. Turn cuffs down.

RIGHT FRONT PLACKET
Row 1: With F hook and Citron, and with right side facing you, attach yarn to right front side at in bottom sc, 1sc in same st as joining, 1sc in each sc up to neck edge. Turn. (79sc)
Rows 2–5: Ch1, 1sc in each sc across. Turn. (79sc) At end of row 5 fasten off and weave in ends.

LEFT FRONT PLACKET
Row 1: With F hook and Citron, and with right side facing you, attach yarn to left front side in top sc, near neck edge, 1sc in same st as joining, 1sc in each sc to bottom edge. Turn. (79sc)
Rows 2–5: Ch1, 1sc in each sc across. Turn. (79sc) Fasten off leaving about an 8" tail to sew with.
Overlap placket bands on top of each other and sew the 5 rows tog at bottom of bands, as shown in picture. With F hook and Summer Sky Heather, attach yarn to bottom right corner of bunting and working across the bottom and working thru both thicknesses, sc tog the bottom of the bunting closed as shown in picture. Using fabric glue, attach Velcro under plackets.

FACE TRIM AND TIES
Row 1: With F hook and citron, attach yarn to st at neckline of hood, 1sc in same st as joining, 1sc in each end of row across to other side of hood. Turn.
Row 2: Ch1, 1sc in the backloops of each sc across. Turn
Rows 3–4: 1sc in each sc across. Turn.
Row 5: Ch41, 1slst in second ch from hook, 1slst in each rem ch, 1sc in next 46sc, ch41, 1slst in second ch from hook, 1slst in each rem ch, slst in same sc. Fasten off and weave in ends.

Step 2: Sew bottom of plackets together, overlapping one on top of the other.

Step 3: Sc along bottom of bunting working thru both thicknesses to close bottom of bunting.

Pretty Posy Petal Body Suit and Hat

0-24 months

Take a walk through the flowers with this lovable pretty posy body suit and hat! Made with soft lightweight yarns, your little one will look perfect among the flowers of spring or summer wearing this fun set.

Materials

- Bernat Softee Baby 5oz/140g/362yds/331m #3 light weight 100% acrylic
– Color number 30221 / color name Soft Fern / 1 skein
– Color number 30301 / color name Baby Pink Marl / 1 skein
– Color number 30205 / color name Prettiest Pink / 1 skein
- Yarn Needle
- Scissors

- **Hooks:** US H (8/5.00mm) and US I (9/5.50mm)

Skill level: Intermediate

Gauge:
I hook = 12dc = 4"
7dc rows = 4.5"

Glossary of abbreviations

ch – chain
dc – double crochet
hdc – half double crochet
picot – slst in top of dc
rnd(s) – round(s)
sc – single crochet
slst – slip stitch

CH3 counts as first dc

0-3 months size written first, body suit = 15" circumference, 9" tall
3-6 months size (in parenthesis), body suit = 17" circumference, 10" tall
6-12 months size (in parenthesis), body suit = 19" circumference, 11" tall
18-24 months size (in parenthesis), body suit = 21" circumference, 12" tall

BODY SUIT

Rnd 1: With I hook and Soft Fern, ch3, 11dc in 3rd ch from hook. Slst to join. (12dc)

Rnd 2: Ch3, 1dc in same st as joining, 2dc in each dc around. Slst to join. (24dc)

Rnd 3: Ch3, 2dc in next dc, (1dc in next dc, 2dc in next dc) rep around. Slst to join. (36dc)

Rnd 4: Ch3, 1dc in each of the next 3dc, ch16 (ch18, ch20, ch22), skip next 9dc, 1dc in each of the next 9dc, ch16 (ch18, ch20, ch22), skip the next 9dc, 1dc in each of the last 5dc. Slst to join.

Rnd 5: Ch3, 1dc in each dc and each ch around. Slst to join. (50dc, 54dc, 58dc, 62dc)

NOTE: Rnds 6–17 (6–18, 6–20, 6–22) work all stitches in backloops

Rnd 6: Ch3, 1dc in dc around. Slst to join. (50dc, 54dc, 58dc, 62dc)

Rnd 7: Ch3, 1dc in each dc around and at the same time decrease rnd by 2dc anywhere on this rnd. Slst to join. (48dc, 52dc, 56dc, 60dc)

Rnd 8: Ch3, 1dc in each dc around. Slst to join. (48dc, 52dc, 56dc, 60dc)

Rnds 9–16: Repeat rnds 7 and 8 alternately. (40dc, 44dc, 48dc, 52dc)

Rnd 17 (17–18, 17–20, 17–22): Ch3, 1dc in each dc around. Slst to join. (40dc, 44dc, 48dc, 52dc)

Rnd 18 (19, 21, 23): Ch1, 1sc in same st as joining, 1sc in next 4sc (5sc, 5sc, 6sc). 1st arm strap: ch20, skip next

10sc (11sc, 12sc, 13sc), 1sc in next 10sc (11sc, 12sc, 13sc). 2nd arm strap: ch20, skip next 10, sc (11sc, 12sc, 13sc), 1sc in next 5sc (5sc, 6sc, 6sc). Slst to join.
Rnd 19 (20, 22, 24): Ch1, working in sc and chains, 1sc in same st as joining, *skip next st, 5sc in next st, skip next st, 1slst in next st* rep from * to * around. Slst to join. Fasten off and weave in ends.

ARM STRAP SCALLOPS
1st arm strap: With I hook and Soft Fern, attach yarn to any st in underarm, 1sc in same st as joining, *skip next st, 5sc in next st, skip next st, 1slst in next st* rep from * to * around, working the 5sc on the opposite side of the chains on the arm straps.
Repeat for 2nd arm strap. Fasten off and weave in ends.

BODY SUIT PETALS
Rnd 1: With I hook and Prettiest Pink, attach yarn to any unworked loop in back of body suit on Rnd 17 (18, 20, 22), 1sc in same st as joining, *1sc in next 3sc, 2sc in next sc* rep from * to * around. Slst to join.
NOTE: don't worry about where the sc count ends. Not important
Rnd 2: Ch1, 1sc in same st as joining, *skip next sc, (1sc, 1hdc, 1dc, ch2, picot, 1dc, 1hdc, 1sc) all in next sc,) skip next sc, 1slst in next sc* rep from * to * around. Fasten off leaving a tail to tack petals down.
Rnd 3: With Baby Pink Marl, skip the next unworked rnd down and attach yarn to the next unworked rnd down, near your ch3. 1sc in that unworked loop, 1sc in next 2unworked loops *2sc in next unworked loop, 1sc in next 3unworked loops * repeat from * to * around. Slst to join.
Rnd 4: Ch1, 1sc in same st as joining, *skip next sc, (1sc, 1hdc, 1dc, ch2, picot, 1dc, 1hdc, 1sc) all in next sc, skip next sc, 1slst in next sc* rep from * to *

Step 1: Working on the first side of straps on the body suit.

Step 2: Where to start work for second arm strap.

around. Fasten off leaving a tail to tack petals down.

Rnd 5: With Prettiest Pink, skip the next unworked rnd down and attach yarn to the next unworked rnd down, near your ch3. 1sc in that unworked loop, 1sc in next 2unworked loops *2sc in next unworked loop, 1sc in next 3unworked loops* repeat from * to * around. Slst to join.

Rnd 6: Ch1, 1sc in same st as joining, *skip next sc, (1sc, 1hdc, 1dc, ch2, picot, 1dc, 1hdc, 1sc) all in next sc, skip next sc, 1slst in next sc* rep from * to * around. Fasten off leaving a tail to tack petals down.

Rnds 7–12 (7–14, 7–16, 7–18): Repeat rnds 3–6 in sequence.

Rnd 13 (15, 17, 19): With Soft Fern and I hook, attach yarn to last unworked rnd in the back of the body suit, 1sc in same st as joining, *skip next sc, 7dc in next sc, skip next sc, 1slst in next sc* rep from * to * around.

BEANIE
0–3 months size 14"
Stem (start of beanie)

Rnd 1: With H hook and Soft Fern, make a magic loop: 6sc inside loop, pull loop tight. Slst to join. (6sc)

Rnd 2: Ch1, 1sc in backloop of same st as joining, 1sc in backloops of each sc around. (6sc) Slst to join.

Rnds 3–4: Ch1, 1sc in same st as joining, 1sc in each sc around. Slst to join. (6sc)

Rnd 5: Ch1, 2sc in same st as joining, 2sc in each sc around. Slst to join. (12sc)

NOTE: ch3 counts as first dc.

Hat Base

Starting with rnd 1 on hat base work all stitches in the back loop.

Rnd 1: Ch3, 1dc in same st as joining, 2dc in each dc around. Slst to join. (24dc)

Rnd 2: Ch3, 2dc in next dc, *1dc in next dc, 2dc in next dc* repeat from *

Step 3: Working on the opposite side of arm strap.

Step 4: Attach first color to first unworked loop round.

to * around. Slst to join. (36dc)
Rnds 3–7: Ch3, 1dc in each dc around. Slst to join. (36dc)
Rnd 8: Ch1, 1sc in same st as joining, *skip 1 sc, 7dc in next sc, skip 1sc, 1sc in next sc* rep from * to * around. Slst to join. Fasten off and tie in ends.

3–6 MONTHS SIZE 15"
Stem (start of beanie)
Rnd 1: With H hook and Soft Fern, make a magic loop: 6sc inside loop, pull loop tight. Slst to join. (6sc)
Rnd 2: Ch1, 1sc in backloop of same st as joining, 1sc in backloops of each sc around. (6sc)Slst to join.
Rnds 3–4: Ch1, 1sc in same st as joining, 1sc in each sc around. Slst to join. (6sc)
Rnd 5: Ch1, 2sc in same st as joining, 2sc in each sc around. Slst to join. (12sc)
NOTE: ch3 counts as first dc.

Hat Base
Starting with rnd 1 on hat base work all stitches in the back loop
Rnd 1: Ch3, 1dc in same st as joining, 2dc in each dc around. Slst to join. (24dc)
Rnd 2: Ch3, 2dc in next dc, *1dc in next dc, 2dc in next dc* repeat from * to * around. Slst to join. (36dc)
Rnd 3: Ch3, dc in next dc, 2dc in next dc, *1dc in next 2dc, 2dc in next dc* repeat from * to * around. Slst to join. (48dc)
Rnds 4–9: Ch3, 1dc in each dc around. Slst to join. (48dc)
Rnd 10: Ch1, 1sc in same st as joining, *skip 1 sc, 7dc in next sc, skip 1sc, 1sc in next sc* rep from * to * around. Slst to join. Fasten off and tie in ends.

6–12 MONTHS SIZE 16"
Stem (start of beanie)
Rnd 1: With H hook and Soft Fern, make a magic loop: 6sc inside loop, pull loop tight. Slst to join. (6sc)
Rnd 2: Ch1, 1sc in backloop of same st

as joining, 1sc in backloops of each sc around. (6sc) Slst to join.
Rnds 3–4: Ch1, 1sc in same st as joining, 1sc in each sc around. Slst to join. (6sc)
Rnd 5: Ch1, 2sc in same st as joining, 2sc in each sc around. Slst to join. (12sc)
NOTE: ch3 counts as first dc.

Hat Base
Starting with rnd 1 on hat base work all stitches in the back loop.
Rnd 1: Ch3, 1dc in same st as joining, 2dc in each dc around. Slst to join. (24dc)
Rnd 2: Ch3, 2dc in next dc, *1dc in next dc, 2dc in next dc* repeat from * to * around. Slst to join. (36dc)
Rnd 3: Ch3, dc in next dc, 2dc in next dc, *1dc in next 2dc, 2dc in next dc* repeat from * to * around. Slst to join. (48dc)
Rnd 4: Ch3, dc in next 6dc, 2dc in next dc, *1dc in next 7dc, 2dc in next dc* repeat from * to * around. Slst to join. (54dc)
Rnds 5–10: Ch3, 1dc in each dc around. Slst to join. (54dc)
Rnd 11: Ch1, 1sc in same st as joining, *skip 1 sc, 7dc in next sc, skip 1sc, 1sc in next sc* rep from * to * around. Slst to join. Fasten off and tie in ends.

18 TO 24 MONTHS SIZE 18"
Stem (start of beanie)
Rnd 1: With H hook and Soft Fern, make a magic loop: 6sc inside loop, pull loop tight. Slst to join. (6sc)
Rnd 2: Ch1, 1sc in backloop of same st as joining, 1sc in backloops of each sc around. Slst to join. (6sc)
Rnds 3–4: Ch1, 1sc in same st as joining, 1sc in each sc around. Slst to join. (6sc)
Rnd 5: Ch1, 2sc in same st as joining, 2sc in each sc around. Slst to join. (12sc)
NOTE: ch3 counts as first dc.

Hat Base
Starting with rnd 1 on hat base work all stitches in the back loop.
Rnd 1: Ch3, 1dc in same st as joining, 2dc in each dc around. Slst to join. (24dc)
Rnd 2: Ch3, 2dc in next dc, *1dc in next dc, 2dc in next dc* repeat from * to * around. Slst to join. (36dc)
Rnd 3: Ch3, dc in next dc, 2dc in next dc, *1dc in next 2dc, 2dc in next dc* repeat from * to * around. Slst to join. (48dc)
Rnd 4: Ch3, dc in next 2dc, 2dc in next dc, *1dc in next 3dc, 2dc in next dc* repeat from * to * around. Slst to join. (60dc)
Rnds 5–12: Ch3, 1dc in each dc around. Slst to join. (60dc)
Rnd 13: Ch1, 1sc in same st as joining, *skip 1 sc, 7dc in next sc, skip 1sc, 1sc in next sc* rep from * to * around. Slst to join. Fasten off and tie in ends.

OUTSIDE PETALS
NOTE: the count doesn't really matter on these petals.
Rnd 1: With I hook and with top of beanie facing you, attach Prettiest Pink to any unworked loop on top of hat on rnd5, sc in joining, *1sc in the next sc, 2sc in the next sc* repeat from * to * around. Slst to join.
Rnd 2: Ch1, 1sc in same st as joining, *skip next sc, (1sc, 1hdc, 1dc, ch2, picot, 1dc, 1hdc, 1sc) all in next sc, skip next sc, 1slst in next sc* rep from * to * around. Fasten off leaving a tail to tack petals down.
Rnd 3: With Baby Pink Marl, skip the next unworked rnd down and attach yarn to the next unworked rnd down, near your ch3. 1sc in that unworked loop, 1sc in next 2 unworked loops *2sc in next unworked loop, 1sc in next 3 unworked loops* repeat from * to * around. Slst to join.
Rnd 4: Ch1, 1sc in same st as joining, *skip next sc, (1sc, 1hdc, 1dc, ch2, picot, 1dc, 1hdc, 1sc) all in next sc, skip

Step 5: First round of petals on hat.

next sc, 1slst in next sc* rep from * to * around. Fasten off leaving a tail to tack petals down.

Rnd 5: With Prettiest Pink, skip the next unworked rnd down and attach yarn to the next unworked rnd down, near your ch3. 1sc in that unworked loop, 1sc in next 2 unworked loops *2sc in next unworked loop, 1sc in next 3 unworked loops* repeat from * to * around. Slst to join.

Rnd 6: Ch1, 1sc in same st as joining, *skip next sc, (1sc, 1hdc, 1dc, ch2, picot, 1dc, 1hdc, 1sc) all in next sc, skip next sc, 1slst in next sc* rep from * to * around. Fasten off leaving a tail to tack petals down.

Rnds 7–8 (7–10, 7–12, 7–14): Repeat rnds 3–6 in sequence. Sew all petals down to hat base.

NOTE: rnds 7–8 Prettiest Pink
rnds 9–10 Baby Pink Marl
rnds 11–12 Prettiest Pink
rnds 13–14 Baby Pink Marl

LEAF – MAKE 2 LEAVES

Rnd 1: With Soft Fern and H hook, ch2, 6sc in second ch from hook. Slst to join.

Rnd 2: 1sc in same st as joining, 1sc in next sc, (1sc, 1hdc, 1dc, ch2, picot, 1hdc, 1dc, 1sc) all in next sc, 1sc in next 3sc. Slst to join. Fasten off leaving a tail to sew with. Attach leaves to top of hat near stem.

Step 6: Second round of petals on hat, tack down petals.

Sock Monkey Hat and Diaper Cover

0-12 months

Your little monkey will look adorable in this stylish sock monkey set.

Materials

- Patons Classic Wool 3.5oz/100g/210yds/192m #4 medium weight 100% wool
- Color number 77251, Color Name Lt Grey Marle / 1 skein
- Color number 00230, Color Name Bright Red / 1 skein
- Color number 00201, Color Name Winter White / 1 skein
- Yarn Needle
- Scissors
- 4 x ½" buttons, for eyes and front of diaper cover

- **Hooks:** US H (8/5.00mm) and US I (9/5.50mm)

Gauge:
H hook = 20sc x 26sc rows = 4"

Skill level: Intermediate

Glossary of abbreviations

ch – chain
dc – double crochet
rem – remaining
rep – repeat
rnd(s) – round(s)
sc – single crochet
slst – slip stitch
tog – together

CH3 counts as first dc

Use H hook to make 0–6 months size hat, 14.4" circumference 5" tall
Use H hook to make 0–6 months size diaper cover, 18" circumference 9" long
Use I hook to make 6–12 months size hat, 15½" circumference, 5½" tall
Use I hook to make 6–12 months size diaper cover, 19" circumference 10½" long

HAT
Start with the pompom
Rnd 1: With H or I hook and Bright Red, ch2, 6sc in second ch from hook. Work in continuous rnds.
Rnd 2: 2sc in each sc around. (12sc)
Rnds 3–4: 1sc in each sc around. (12sc)
Rnd 5: (sc tog the next 2sc) rep 5 more times. (6sc)
Rnd 6: 2sc in each sc around. (12sc)
Rnd 7: 2sc in each sc around. (24sc)
Rnd 8: *1sc in the next sc, 2sc in next sc* rep from * to * around. (36sc)
Rnd 9: *1sc in the next 2sc, 2sc in next sc* rep from * to * around. (48sc)

Fasten off Bright Red
Rnd 10: With H or I hook, and Winter White, attach to where you fastened off, 1sc in same st as joining, 1sc in each sc around. Slst to join. (48sc)
Rnd 11: Ch1, 1sc in same st as joining, 1sc in each sc around. Slst to join. (48sc)
Fasten off Winter White

Head
Rnd 1: With H or I hook and Lt Grey Marle, attach yarn to where you fastened off. 1Sc in same st as joining, 1sc in each sc around. Slst to join.

Turn. (48sc)
Rnds 2–8: Ch1, 1sc in each sc around. Slst to join. Turn. (48sc)

First Earflap
Row 1: 1sc in each of the next 12sc. Turn.
Rows 2–3: Ch1, 1sc in each of the next 6sc. Turn, (6sc) leaving rest of row unworked for now.
Row 4: Ch1, sc tog the first 2sc, 1sc in next 2sc, sc tog the last 2sc. Turn. (4sc)
Row 5: Ch1, 1sc in each sc across. Turn. (4sc)
Row 6: Ch1, (sc tog the next 2sc) rep

Step 1: Sew on ears.

Step 2: Sew on mouth.

one more time. Turn. (2sc)

Row 7: Ch1, sc tog the last 2sc. Slst down left side of earflap back to last rnd of hat. 1sc in each of the next (24sc) Turn.

Second Earflap

Rows 1–2: 1sc in each of the next 6sc. Turn. (6sc)

Row 3: Ch1, sc tog the first 2sc, 1sc in next 2sc, sc tog the last 2sc. Turn. (4sc)

Row 4: Ch1, 1sc in each sc across. Ch1, turn. (4sc)

Row 5:Ch1, (sc tog the next 2sc) rep one more time. Turn. (2sc)

Row 6: Ch1, sc tog the last 2sc. Slst down left side of earflap back to last rnd of hat. 1Sc in each sc to end of rnd. Slst to join. Ch1. Do not turn.

Trims

Rnd 1: 1sc in each sc and each st around each earflap. Slst to join.

Rnd 2: 1sc in each sc around. When you get to the bottom middle of each earflap, (sc, ch3, sc) in each end. Finish rnd and slst to join. Fasten off and weave in ends.

Braids

Cut 2 strands of each color to desired length and pull thru ch3 loops at tips of each earflap. Braid all the strands together.

Mouth

Rnd 1: With H hook and Winter White, ch7, 2sc in second ch from hook, 1sc in each of the next 4ch, 3sc in last ch. Now working on the other side of the chain, 1sc in each of the next 4ch, 1sc in same st as beg. Slst to join. Ch1. (14sc) Fasten off leaving a tail to sew the mouth onto the hat with. Sew mouth over last 2rnds on hat in middle front of face.

Embroider a Bright Red mouth over stitches by making 2 vertical lines on each end and a horizontal line in middle for smile.

Ears – make 2

Row 1: With H hook and Lt Grey Marle. Ch2, 6sc in second ch from hook. Slst to join. Turn. (6sc)

Row 2: 1sc in next sc, 2sc in each of the next 4sc, 1sc in last sc. Do not join. Turn. (10sc)

Row 3: Ch1, 1sc in next 10sc, 1sc across ends of rows on bottom of ear. Slst to join. Fasten off leaving a tail to sew with. Attach ears to front of hat right before earflaps.

Sew buttons on for eyes right above where the mouth is.

DIAPER COVER

Use H hook to make 0–6 months size. Use I hook to make 6–12 months size.

Row 1: With H or I hook and Lt Grey Marle, ch 53, 1sc in second ch from hook, 1sc in each rem ch. Turn. (52sc)

Note: ch2 counts as first dc.

Row 2: Ch2, 1dc in each dc across. Turn. (52dc)

Row 3: Ch1, slst across first 19dc, 1sc in each of the next 14dc, leave the rest of the row unworked. Turn. (14sc)

Rows 4–10: Ch, 1sc in each sc across. Turn. (14sc)

Row 11: Ch1, sc tog the next 2sc, 1sc in each sc to last 2sc, sc tog the last 2sc. Turn. (12sc)

Row 12: Ch1, 1sc in each sc across. Turn. (12sc)

Row 13: Ch1, sc tog the next 2sc, 1sc in each sc to last 2sc, sc tog the last 2sc. Turn. (10sc)

Row 14: Ch1, 1sc in each sc across. Turn. (10sc)

Rows 15–18: Ch1, 1sc in each sc across. Turn. (10sc)

Row 19: Ch1, 2sc in next sc, 1sc in each sc across row to last sc, 2sc in next sc. Turn. (12sc)

Rows 20–21: Ch1, 1sc in each sc across. Turn. (12sc)

Row 22: Repeat row 19 (14sc)

Rows 23–26: Repeat row 20. At end of row 26 do not fasten off but continue on to instructions for trim.

Step 3: Weave strands through hole in bottom of earflap.

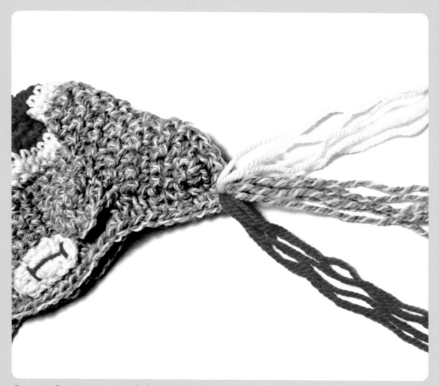

Step 4: Separate strands by color.

Trim

Rnd1: 1sc in each end of row and st around entire diaper cover. Slst to join. Fasten off, weave in ends.

Rnd 2: With H or I hook and Winter White, attach yarn to any stitch. 1sc in each sc around entire diaper cover. Slst to join. Fasten off and weave in ends.

Rnd 3: With H or I hook and Bright Red, attach yarn to where you fastened off, 1sc in same st as joining, 1sc in each sc around. Slst to join. Fasten off and weave in ends.

Finishing: attach buttons to front flap.

Step 5: Braid strands together.

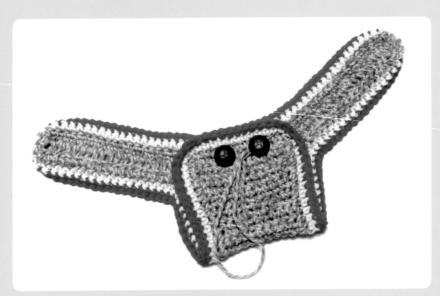

Step 6: Sew buttons on diaper cover.

Cable Hooded Cardigan

Made with super soft acrylic yarn, this cardigan sweater is sure to keep your little one warm and cozy.

Materials

- Cascade Cherub Aran 3.5oz/100g/240yds/220m #4 medium weight 55%Nylon, 45%Acrylic
– Color number 35 / color name Taupe / 3 skeins
- 4 x 5/8" buttons
- Yarn Needle
- Scissors

- **Hook:** US I (9/5.50mm)

Gauge:
I hook: 4" x 4" – 12sc x 15rows

Skill level: Intermediate

Glossary of abbreviations

ch – chain
chsp – chain space
corner – (1sc, ch2, 1sc) all in same st
dc – double crochet
fpdc – front post double crochet: yo, insert hook under dc post, yo, bring yarn back thru, yo, drop off first 2loops, yo, drop off last 2loops.
fptrc – front post treble crochet or triple crochet – yo twice, insert hook under dc post, yo, bring yarn back thru, yo, drop off first 2loops, yo, drop off next 2loops, yo, drop off last 2loops.
prev – previous
rnd(s) – round(s)sc – single crochet
st – stitch
trc – treble crochet, yo twice, insert hook in next st, bring yarn back thru, (yo, drop off first 2loops) rep 2 more times.
yo – yarn over hook

NOTE: To make buttonholes: ch1, skip next sc, 1sc in next sc.
To make the twist in the cables: skip next 2fpdc, 1fptrc around 3rd fpdc, 1fptrc around 4th fpdc, now go back to the first fpdc, 1fptrc around first fpdc, 1fptrc around second fpdc.

0–3 months size measurements: Chest 19"; from neck edge to tip of sleeve: sleeve length 7"; underarm to bottom of sweater 7.5"; hood 6.5" tall
3–6 months size measurements: Chest 20"; from neck edge to tip of sleeve: sleeve length 8"; underarm to bottom of sweater 8.5"; hood 7.5" tall
Instructions are written for 0–3 months size and the 3–6 months size are in parenthesis.

HOODED CARDIGAN
Yoke
Row 1: With I hook and Taupe, ch29 (34), 1sc in second ch from hook, 1sc in next 3ch (4ch), (1sc, ch2, 1sc) in next ch, 1sc in next 4ch (5ch), (1sc, ch2, 1sc) in next ch, 1sc in next 8ch (9ch), (1sc, ch2, 1sc) in next ch, 1sc in next 4ch (5ch), (1sc, ch1, 1sc) in next ch, 1sc in last 4ch (5ch). Turn. (32sc and 4ch2sps)

(37sc and 4 ch2sps)
Row 2: Ch1, 1sc in next 5sc (6sc), corner in next chsp, 1sc in next 6sc (7sc), corner in next chsp, 1sc in next 10sc (11sc), corner in next chsp, 1sc in next 6sc (7sc), corner in next chsp, 1sc in next 5sc (6sc). Turn. (40sc and 4ch2sps) (45sc and 4ch2sps)
Row 3: Ch1, 1sc in next 6sc (7sc), corner in next chsp, 1sc in next 8sc

(9sc), corner in next chsp, 1sc in next 12sc (13sc), corner in next chsp, 1sc in next 8sc (9sc), corner in next chsp, 1sc in next 6sc (7sc). Turn. (48sc and 4ch2sps) (53sc and 4ch2sp)
Row 4: Ch1, 1sc in next 7sc (8sc),

Step 1: Front post double crochet (fpdc).

Step 2: Fpdc around post of fpdc 2 rows below.

corner in next chsp, 1sc in next 10sc (11sc), corner in next chsp, 1sc in next 14sc (15sc), corner in next chsp, 1sc in next 10sc (11sc), corner in next chsp, 1sc in next 7sc (8sc). Turn. (56sc and 4ch2sps) (61sc and 4ch2sps)

Row 5: Ch1, 1sc in next 8sc (9sc), corner in next chsp, 1sc in next 12sc (13sc), corner in next chsp, 1sc in next 16sc (17sc), corner in next chsp, 1sc in next 12sc (13sc), corner in next chsp, 1sc in next 8sc (9sc). Turn. (64sc and 4ch2sps) (69sc and 4ch2sps)

Row 6: Ch1, 1sc in next 9sc (10sc), corner in next chsp, 1sc in next 14sc (15sc), corner in next chsp, 1sc in next 18sc (19sc), corner in next chsp, 1sc in next 14sc (15sc), corner in next chsp, 1sc in next 9sc (10sc). Turn. (72sc and 4ch2sps) (77sc and 4ch2sps)

Row 7: Ch1, 1sc in next 10sc (11sc), corner in next chsp, 1sc in next 16sc (17sc), corner in next chsp, 1sc in next 20sc (21sc), corner in next chsp, 1sc in next 16sc (17sc), corner in next chsp, 1sc in next 10sc (11sc). Turn. (80sc and 4ch2sps) (85sc and 4ch2sps)

Row 8: Ch1, 1sc in next 11sc (12sc), corner in next chsp, 1sc in next 18sc (19sc), corner in next chsp, 1sc in next 22sc (23sc), corner in next chsp, 1sc in next 18sc (19sc), corner in next chsp, 1sc in next 11sc (12sc). Turn. (88sc and 4ch2sps) (93sc and 4ch2sps)

Stop here for the 0–3 months size and continue on to Underarms and body section.

Size 3–6 months only:

Row 9: Ch1, 1sc in next 13sc, corner in next chsp, 1sc in next 21sc corner in next chsp, 1sc in next 25sc, corner in next chsp, 1sc in next 21sc, corner in next chsp, 1sc in next 13sc Turn. (88sc and 4ch2sps) (101sc and 4ch2sps)

Row 10: Ch1, 1sc in next 14sc, corner in next chsp, 1sc in next 23sc corner in next chsp, 1sc in next 27sc. corner in next chsp, 1sc in next 23sc corner in next chsp, 1sc in next 14sc Turn. (88sc

and 4ch2sps) (109sc and 4ch2sps)

Both sizes – underarms and body

Row 1: Ch1, 1sc in next 12sc (15sc), 1sc in next ch2sp, ch4, skip next 20sc (25sc), 1sc in next ch2sp, 1sc in next 24sc (29sc), 1sc in next ch2sp, ch4, skip next 20sc (25sc), 1sc in next ch2sp, 1sc in next 12sc (15sc). Turn. (52sc and 8ch) (63sc and 8ch)

Row 2: Ch1, 1sc in each sc and in each ch across. Turn. (60sc) (71sc)

Row 3: Ch1, 1sc in next 3sc, 1dc in next 4sc, *1sc in next 2sc, 1dc in next 2sc, 1sc in next 2sc, 1dc in next 4sc* rep from * to * across, ending with 1sc in last 3sc (4sc). Turn. (60sts) (71sts)

Row 4: Ch1, 1sc in each st across. Turn. (60sc) (71sc)

Row 5: Ch1, 1sc in next 3sc, 1fpdc around next 4dc, *2sc in next sc, 1sc in next sc, 1fpdc around next 2dc, 2sc in next sc,1sc in next sc, 1fpdc around next 4dc* rep from * to * across ending with 1sc in last 3sc(4sc). Turn. (70sts) (83sts)

Row 6: Ch1, 1sc in each st across. Turn. (70sc) (83sc)

Row 7: 1sc in next 3sc, 1fpdc around next 4fpdc, *1sc in next sc, 2sc in next sc, 1sc in next sc, 1fpdc around next 2fpdc, 1sc in next sc, 2sc in next sc, 1sc in next sc, 1fpdc around next 4fpdc* rep from * to * across ending with 1sc in last 3sc (4sc). Turn. (80sts) (95sts)

Row 8: Ch1, 1sc in each st across. Turn. (80sc) (95sc)

Row 9: Ch1, 1sc in next 3sc, (1st twist) skip next 2fpdc, 1fptrc around 3rd fpdc, 1fptrc around 4th fpdc, 1fptrc around 1st fpdc, 1fptrc around 2nd fpdc, *1sc in next sc, 2sc in next sc, 1sc in next 2sc, 1fpdc around next 2fpdc, 1sc in next sc, 2sc in next sc, 1sc in next 2sc, twist* rep from * to * across ending with 1sc in last 3sc (4sc). Turn. (90sts) (107sts)

Row 10: Ch1, 1sc in each st across. Turn. (90sc) (107sc)

Row 11: Ch1, 1sc in next 3sc, 1fpdc

Step 3: First fptrc for twist in cables.

Step 4: Second fptrc for twist in cables.

Step 5: Third fptrc for twist in cables.

Step 6: Fourth fptrc for twist in cables.

around next 4fptrc, *1sc in next 5sc, 1fpdc around next 2fpdc, 1sc in next 5sc, 1fpdc around next 4fptrc* rep from * to * across, ending with 1sc in last 3sc (4sc). Turn. (90sts) (107sts)

Row 12: Repeat row 10. (90sc) (107sc)

Row 13: 1sc in next 3sc, 1fpdc around next 4fpdc, *1sc in next 5sc, 1fpdc around next 2fpdc, 1sc in next 5sc, 1fpdc around next 4fpdc* rep from * to * across ending with 1sc in last 3sc (4sc). Turn. (90sts) (107sts)

Row 14: Repeat row 10. (90sc) (107sts)

Row 15: 1sc in next 3sc, 1fpdc around next 4fpdc, *1sc in next 5sc, 1fpdc around next 2fpdc, 1sc in next 5sc, 1fpdc around next 4fpdc* rep from * to * across ending with 1sc in last 3sc (4sc). Turn. (90sts) (107sts)

Row 16: Ch1, 1sc in each st across. Turn. (90sc) (107sts)

Row 17: Ch1, 1sc in next 3sc, twist, *1sc in next 5sc, 1fpdc around next 2fpdc, 1sc in next 5sc, twist* rep from * to * across ending with 1sc in last 3sc (4sc). Turn. (90sts) (107sts)

Row 18: Ch1, 1sc in each st across. Turn. (90sc) (107sts)

Row 19: 1sc in next 3sc, 1fpdc around next 4fptrc, *1sc in next 5sc, 1fpdc around next 2fpdc, 1sc in next 5sc, 1fpdc around next 4fptrc* rep from * to * across ending with 1sc in last 3sc (4sc). Turn. (90sts) (107sts)

Row 20: Ch1, 1sc in each st across. Turn. (90sc) (107sts)

Rows 21–27 (21–35): Repeat rows 13–19 in sequence, at end of row 27 (35) turn to work in ends of rows on front of sweater.

NOTE: girls' buttonholes go on right side of sweater, boys' buttonholes on left side of sweater.

PLACKET

Row 1: 1sc in each of the next 3 ends of rows, (skip next end of row, 1sc in next 3 ends of rows) rep to neck edge. Turn.

Rows 2–3: Ch1, 1sc in each sc across. Turn.

NECK

Row 1: 1sc in each st across neck edge over to left front of sweater.
Buttonhole Placket
Row 1: 1sc in each of the next 3 ends of rows, (skip next end of row, 1sc in each of the next 3 ends of row) rep to bottom edge. Turn.
Row 2: Ch1, 1sc in each sc, across, and at the same time make 4 buttonholes evenly spaced across the row. Turn.
Row 3: Ch1, 1sc in each sc and in each chsp. Fasten off and weave in ends.

SLEEVES – MAKE 2

Row 1: With I hook and Taupe, attach yarn to bottom of arm opening on the inside or wrong side of sleeve, 1sc in same st as joining, 1sc in each st around. Slst to join. Turn. (24sc) (31sc)
Row 2: Ch1, 1sc in same st as joining, 1sc in next 4sc (10sc), 1dc in next 2sc, 1sc in next 3sc, 1dc in next 4sc, 1sc in next 3sc, 1dc in next 2sc, 1sc in next 5sc (6sc). Slst to join. Turn. (24sts) (31sts)
Row 3: Ch1, 1sc in same st as joining, 1sc in each st around. Slst to join. Turn. (24sc) (31sc)
Row 4: Ch1, 1sc in same st as joining, 1sc in next 4sc (10sc), 1fpdc around next 2dc, 1sc in next 3sc, 1fpdc around next 4dc, 1sc in next 3sc, 1fpdc around next 2dc, 1sc in last 5sc. Slst to join. Turn. (24sts) (31sts)
Row 5: Repeat row 3. (24sc) (31sc)
Row 6: Ch1, 1sc in same st as joining, 1sc in next 4sc (10sc), 1fpdc around next 2fpdc, *1sc in next 3sc, 1fpdc around next 4fpdc, 1sc in next 3sc, 1fpdc around next 2fpdc, 1sc in last 5sc (6sc). Slst to join. Turn. (24sts) (31sts)
Row 7: Repeat row 3. (24sc) (31sc)
Row 8: Ch1, 1sc in same st as joining, 1sc in next 4sc (10sc), 1fpdc around next 2fpdc, 1sc in next 3sc, twist, 1sc in next 3sc, 1fpdc around next 2fpdc, 1sc in last 5sc (6sc). Slst to join. Turn. (24sts) (31sts)
Row 9: Repeat row 3. (24sc) (31sc)
Row 10: Ch1, 1sc in same st as joining, 1sc in next 4sc (10sc), 1fpdc around next 2fpdc, 1sc in next 3sc, 1fpdc

Step 7: Fold hood in half, sc across top, working thru both thicknesses to close top of hood.

around next 4fptrc, 1sc in next 3sc, 1sc in last 5sc (6sc). Slst to join. Turn. (24sts) (31sts)

Row 11: Repeat row 3. (24sc) (31sc)

Row 12: Ch1, 1sc in same st as joining, 1sc in next 4sc (10sc), 1fpdc around next 2fpdc, 1sc in next 3sc, 1fpdc around next 4fpdc, 1sc in next 3sc, 1sc in last 5sc (6sc). Slst to join. Turn. (24sts) (31sts)

Row 13: Repeat row 3. (24sc) (31sc)

Row 14: Ch1, 1sc in same st as joining, 1sc in next 4sc (10sc), 1fpdc around next 2fpdc, 1sc in next 3sc, 1fpdc around next 4fpdc, 1sc in next 3sc, 1sc in last 5sc (6sc). Slst to join. Turn. (24sts) (31sts)

Row 15: Repeat row 3. (24sc) (31sc)

Row 16: Ch1, 1sc in same st as joining, 1sc in next 4sc (10sc), 1fpdc around next 2fpdc, 1sc in next 3sc, twist, 1sc in next 3sc, 1fpdc around next 2fpdc, 1sc in last 5sc (6sc). Slst to join. Turn. (24sts) (31sts)

Rows 17–23 (17–30): Repeat rows 10–16 in sequence.

Row 24 (31): Ch1, 1sc in same st as joining, sc tog the next 2sts, (1sc in next st, sc tog the next 2sc) rep around. (For larger size, end with 1sc in last st.) Slst to join. (16sc) (21sc)

Rows 25–28 (32–36): Ch1, 1sc in same st as joining, 1sc in each sc around. Slst to join. (16sc) (21sc) At end of row 28 (36) fasten off and weave in ends.

HOOD

Row 1: With I hook and Taupe, and with inside of sweater facing you, attach yarn to 8th (9th) st from the right on neck edge, 2sc in same st as joining, 2sc in each sc across, leaving the last 8sts (9sts) unworked. Turn. (40sc) (46sc)

Row 2: Ch1, 1sc in next 3sc, 1dc in next 2sc, *1sc in next sc, 1dc in next 4sc, 1sc in next sc, 1dc in next 2sc* rep from * to * across, ending with 1sc in last 3sc (4sc). Turn. (40sts) (46sts)

Row 3: Ch1, 1sc in each st across. Turn. (40sc) (46sc)

Row 4: Ch1, 1sc in next 3sc, 1fpdc around next 2dc, *2sc in next sc, 1fpdc around next 4dc, 2sc in next sc, 1fpdc around next 2dc* rep from * to * across, ending with 1sc in last 3sc (4sc). Turn. (48sts) (55sts)

Row 5: Ch1, 1sc in each st across. Turn. (48sc) (55sc)

Row 6: 1sc in next 3sc, 1fpdc around next 2fpdc, *1sc in next 2sc, 1fpdc around next 4fpdc, 1sc in next 2sc, 1fpdc around next 2fpdc* rep from * to * across, ending with 1sc in last 3sc (4sc). Turn. (48sts) (55sts)

Row 7: Repeat row 5. (48sc) (55sc)

Row 8: Ch1, 1sc in next 3sc, 1fpdc around next 2fpdc, *1sc in next 2sc, twist, 1sc in next 2sc, 1fpdc around next 2fpdc* rep from * to * across, ending with 1sc in last 3sc. Turn. (48sts) (55sts)

Row 9: Repeat row 5 (48sc) (55sc)

Row 10: Ch1, 1sc in next 3sc, 1fpdc around next 2fpdc, *1sc in next 2sc, 1fpdc around next 4fptrc, 1sc in next 2sc, 1fpdc around next 2fpdc* rep from * to * across, ending with 1sc in last 3sc (4sc). Turn. (48sts) (55sts)

Row 11: Repeat row 5. (48sc) (55sc)

Row 12: 1sc in next 3sc, 1fpdc around next 2fpdc, *1sc in next 2sc, 1fpdc around next 4fpdc, 1sc in next 2sc, 1fpdc around next 2fpdc* rep from * to * across, ending with 1sc in last 3sc (4sc). Turn. (48sts) (55sts)

Row 13: Repeat row 5 (48sc) (55sc)

Rows 14–20: Repeat rows 6–12.

Row 21: Repeat row 5 (49sc) (55sc)

Rows 22–24: Repeat rows 6, 7 and 8. For 0–3 months size stop here and follow instructions for joining the top of the hood.

For 3-6 months size only

Rows 25–28: Repeat rows 9–12

Rows 29–30: Repeat rows 7 and 8.

Joining Top of Hood

At end of row 24 (30) fasten off and fold hood in half, wrong side facing you. Sc tog the top of hood. Fasten off and weave in end. Turn hood to right side. Fold the front stitches around face of opening of hood and tack in place if desired. Sew buttons on securely.

Cocoons

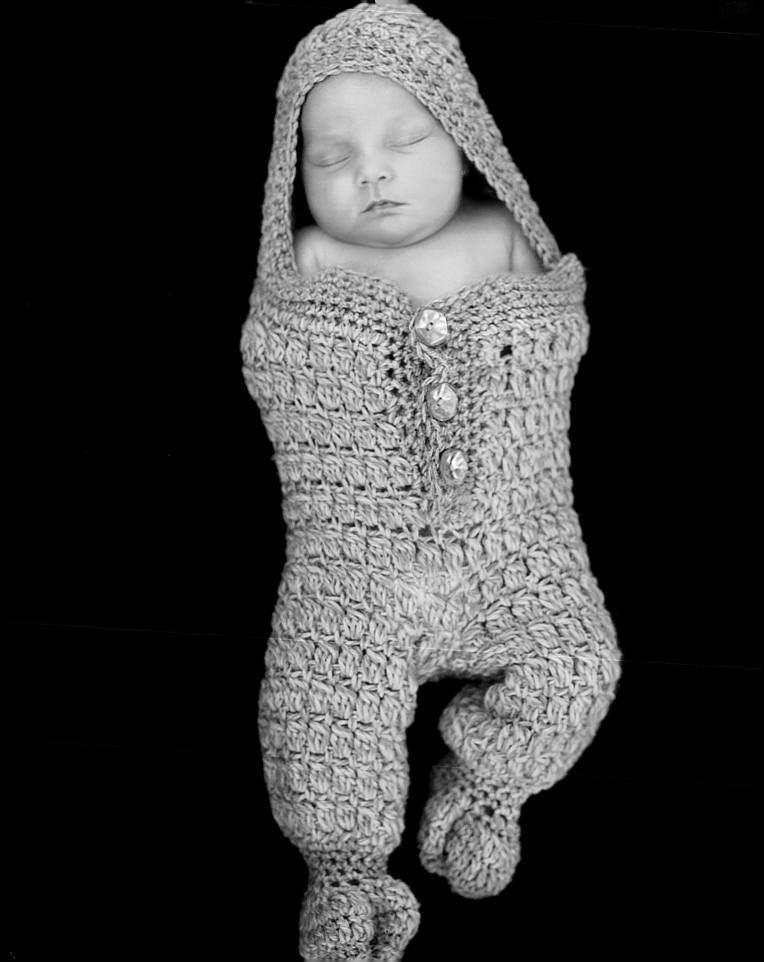

Car Seat Baby Cocoon

0–3 months

This attractive little cocoon is great for strapping into a car seat or stroller. It will keep baby warm and feeling snuggled.

Materials

- Cascade Yarns Quatro 3.5oz/100g/220yds #4 medium weight 100% Peruvian Highland Wool
  - Color number 5011 / color name Orange Twist / 2 skeins
- Cascade Yarns Pure Alpaca 3.5oz/100g/220yds/200m #4 medium weight 100% baby alpaca
  - Color number 3022 / color name Summer Sky Heather / 1 skein
- 3 x 1½" buttons
- Yarn Needle
- Scissors

- **Hooks:** US G (7/4.50mm) and US H (8/5.00mm)

Skill level: Intermediate

Gauge:
1 cluster – 1" tall,
4 clusters – 2" across

Glossary of abbreviations

ch – chain
Cluster – yo, insert hook into ch1sp, pull yarn back thru, yo, drop off first 2 loops, yo, insert hook into same ch1sp, bring yarn back thru, yo, drop off first 2 loops, yo, insert hook into same ch1sp, bring yarn back thru, yo, drop off first 2 loops, yo, drop off all 4 loops on hook.
dc – double crochet
hdc – half double crochet
rep – repeat
rnd(s) – round(s)
sc – single crochet
sk – skip
slst – slip stitch
st – stitch
tog – together
yo – yarn over hook

0–3 months = Measures approximately 23" from bottom of foot to top of hood:

BOOTEES AND LEGS – MAKE 2
Sole
Rnd 1: With H hook and Summer Sky Heather, ch8, (heel) 2sc in second ch from hook, 1sc in next 5ch, (toe) 5sc in last ch. Now working on opposite side of ch, 1sc in next 5ch, 1sc in same ch as beg. Slst to join. (18sc)
Rnd 2: Ch1, 2sc in same st as joining, 2sc in next sc, 1sc in next 5sc, 2sc in next 5sc, 1sc in next 5sc, 2sc in last sc. Slst to join. (26sc)
Rnd 3: Ch1, 2sc in same st as joining, 1sc in next sc, 2sc in next sc, 1sc in next 6sc, (1sc in next sc, 2sc in next sc) rep 4 more times, 1sc in next 6sc, 2sc in last sc. Slst to join. (34sc)

Rnd 4: Ch1, 1sc in the back loop of same st as joining, 1sc in the back loop of each sc around. Slst to join. (34sc) Fasten off Summer Sky Heather.

Side of Bootees
Rnd 1: With H hook and Orange Twist, attach yarn to middle back of bootee, 1sc in same st as joining, 1sc in next 5sc, 1hdc in next 3sc, 1dc in next 20sc, 1hdc in next 3sc, 1sc in next 2sc around. Continue in a spiral fashion. (34sts)
Rnd 2: 1sc in next 6sc, 1hdc in next 3hdc, (dc tog the next 2dc) rep 9 more times, 1hdc in next 3hdc, 1sc in next 2sc. (24sts)
Rnd 3: 1sc in next 6sts, (sc tog the next

2dc) rep 7 more times, 1sc in next 2sc. (16sc)
Rnds 4–6: 1sc in each sc around. (16sc)
Rnd 7: 2sc in each sc around. Slst into next sc. Turn. (32sc)

Start of Leg
Row 1: Ch1, 1sc in same st as joining, ch1,*sk next sc, 1sc in next sc, ch1* rep from * to * around. Slst to join. Turn. (32sts)

Step 1: Connecting legs.

Step 2: Connecting to leg with cluster. first part of cluster.

Row 2: Ch 1, cluster in first ch1 sp, ch1, *sk next sc, cluster in next ch1sp, ch1* rep from * to * around. Slst to top of first cluster to join. Turn. (16clusters)

Row 3: Ch1, 1sc in next ch1sp, ch1, *sk next cluster, 1sc in next ch1sp, ch1* rep from * to * around. Slst to first sc to join. Turn. (32sts)

Row 4: Ch 1, cluster in first ch1 sp, ch1, *sk next sc, cluster in next ch1sp, ch1* rep from * to * around. Slst to top of first cluster to join. Turn. (16clusters)

Row 5: Ch1, 1sc in next ch1sp, ch1, *sk next cluster, 1sc in next ch1sp, ch1* rep from * to * around. Slst to first sc to join. Turn. (32sts)

Rows 6–11: Repeat rows 4 and 5 alternately. At end of row 11, fasten off first leg, do not fasten off for second leg but continue on to cocoon body.

COCOON

Row 1: Ch 1, cluster in first ch1 sp, ch1, *sk next sc, cluster in next ch1sp, ch1* rep from * to * 4 more times, pick up second leg hold the toe of the bootee straight forward, find the next ch1sp on second leg that would be in sequence to make next cluster, cluster in that ch1sp, ch1, *sk next sc, cluster in next ch1sp, ch1* rep from * to * around second leg, slst in top of first cluster on second leg, slst into top of 5th cluster from first leg, ch1, turn, cluster in next ch1sp, *sk next sc, cluster in next ch1sp, ch1* rep from * to * around. Slst to top of first cluster to join. Turn. (32clusters)

Row 2: Ch1, 1sc in next ch1sp, ch1, *sk next cluster, 1sc in next ch1sp, ch1* rep from * to * around. Slst to first sc to join. Turn. (64sts)

Row 3: Ch 1, cluster in first ch1 sp, ch1, *sk next sc, cluster in next ch1sp, ch1* rep from * to * around. Slst to top of first cluster to join. Turn. (32clusters)

Row 4: Repeat row 2.

Row 5: Repeat row 3.

Row 6: Repeat row 2. At end of row fasten off.

Row 7: With H hook and Orange Twist, find the front middle cluster, attach yarn to the ch1sp to the left of the middle cluster, ch1, 1cluster in same ch1sp, ch1, *sk next sc, cluster in next ch1sp, ch1* rep from * to * 29 more times. Turn. (31clusters)

Row 8: Ch1, 1sc in top of first cluster, 1sc in next ch1sp, ch1, *sk next cluster, 1sc in next ch1sp, ch1* rep from * to * across, ending with skip last cluster, 1sc in end st. Turn. (62sts)

Row 9: Ch1, cluster in first ch1 sp, ch1, *sk next sc, cluster in next ch1sp, ch1* rep from * to * across, ending with 1cluster in last sc. Turn. (31clusters)

Row 10: Ch1, 1sc in top of first cluster, 1sc in next ch1sp, ch1, *sk next cluster, 1sc in next ch1sp, ch1* rep from * to * across, ending with skip last cluster, 1sc in end st. Turn. (62sts)

Rows 11–16: Repeat rows 9 and 10 alternately.

Start of Hood

Row 1: Ch1, slst in each of the next 13sts, ch1, cluster in next ch1sp, ch1, *skip next sc, cluster in next ch1sp, ch1* rep from * to * 16 more times, leaving the last 16sts unworked. Turn. (18clusters)

Row 2: Ch1, 1sc in top of first cluster, 1sc in next ch1sp, ch1, *sk next cluster, 1sc in next ch1sp, ch1* rep from * to * across, ending with skip last cluster, 1sc in end st. Turn. (36sts)

Row 3: Ch1, cluster in first ch1 sp, ch1, *sk next sc, cluster in next ch1sp, ch1* rep from * to * across, ending with 1cluster in last sc. Turn. (18clusters)

Rows 4–16: Repeat rows 2 and 3 alternately. At end of row 16 fold row in half and sc across the sts to close the hood. Then slst in each sc back to face of hood. Do not fasten off but continue on to the trim on front of hood and cocoon.

Step 3: Connecting back to the first leg.

Step 4: Leaving 2 clusters unworked in front of cocoon for front plackets to be added in later.

Step 5: Sc tog the top of the hood together, working thru both thicknesses.

Trim
Turn hood to the right side, ch1, 1sc in each end of row around face of hood and down front opening of cocoon. Slst to join. Fasten off Orange Twist.

Trim and Button Plackets
Row 1: With G hook and Summer Sky Heather, attach yarn to sc on right side of cocoon. There are 2sc in middle opening for the button plackets. Attach yarn to first sc. (see photo). 1sc in each sc around entire opening of front cocoon and hood, working to bottom of opening on left side of cocoon. Turn.
Rows 2–3: Ch1, 1sc in each sc on front of cocoon and around hood, working 2sc in corner sc on next edge. Turn.
Row 4: Ch1, 1sc in next 3sc, (buttonhole) ch2, sk next sc, 1sc in next 8sc, (buttonhole) ch2, sk next sc, 1sc in next 8sc, (buttonhole) ch2, sk next sc, 2sc in corner sc, 1sc in each sc around hood and over to other side of button plackets. Turn.
Row 5: Ch1, 1sc in each sc around and 1sc in each ch2sp. Fasten off leaving a tail to sew with.
Sew button placket over the 2sc on bottom of opening as shown in picture. Hold buttonhole placket over the button placket and sew the end down as shown in pictures. Weave in ends.
Sew buttons onto button placket.

Step 6: Where to start button placket.

Step 7: Where to end buttonhole placket.

Step 8: Overlapping the buttonhole placket over the button placket. Sew bottom stitches together.

Step 9: Overlap the buttonhole placket on top of button placket.

Three Peas in a Pod Cocoon and Beanie Set

0-24months

Cozy little peas cocoon for your little sweet pea. Great to use in prop photography.

Materials

- Red Heart Super Saver 7oz/198g/364yds/333m #4 medium weight 100% acrylic
  - Color number 0672 / color name Spring Green / 2 skeins
  - Color number 368 / color name Paddy Green / 1 skein
  - Color number 319 / color name Cherry Red / 1yd
- Polyester fiberfil / small amount
- Yarn Needle
- Scissors

- **Hook:** US I (9/5.00mm)

Gauge:
I hook – 8hdc – 3", 4hdc rows – 2"

Skill level: Intermediate

Glossary of abbreviations

ch – chain
hdc – half double crochet
rem – remaining
rep – repeat
rnd(s) – round(s)
(RS) – right side
sc – single crochet
slst – slip stitch
tog – together
trc – treble crochet, yo twice, insert hook in next st, bring yarn back thru, (yo, drop off first 2loops) rep 2 more times.
yo – yarn over hook

Finished Cocoon measures approximately 17" long x 22" circumference

COCOON

Rnd 1: With Spring Green and I hook, ch 2, 6sc in second ch from hook. Work in continuous rnds. (6sc)
Rnd 2: 2sc in each sc around. (12sc)
Rnd 3: 2sc in each sc around. (24sc)
Rnd 4: *1sc in next sc, 2sc in next sc* rep from * to * around. (36sc)
Rnd 5: 1sc in each sc around. (36sc)
Rnd 6: *1sc in next 2sc, 2sc in next sc* rep from * to * around. (48sc)
Rnd 7: 1sc in each sc around. (48sc)
Rnd 8: *1sc in next 3sc, 2sc in next sc* rep from * to * around. (60sc)
Rnd 9: 1sc in each sc around. (60sc)
Rnds 10–11: 1sc in each sc around. (60sc)

Rnd 12: 1hdc in each sc around. Slst to join. Turn. (60hdc)
NOTE: rnds 13–22: insert hook under the loops of the hdc and work in between the posts of the hdc stitches. This makes a smoother look to your cocoon.
Ch1 does not count as first hdc.
Rnds 13–22: Ch1, 1hdc in between each hdc around. Slst to join. Turn. (60hdc)
You now are going to work in rows.
Row 1: 1hdc in between each of the next 50hdc around. Turn. (50hdc)
Leaving the rest of the row unworked.
Rows 2–23: Ch1, 1hdc in between each of the next 50 hdc. Turn. (50hdc) or

until cocoon measures approximately 16" long.

TRIM

Rnd 1: (RS) 1sc in next 50sc, 1sc in next 23 ends of rows, 1sc in next 10hdc, 1sc in next 23 ends of rows. Slst to join. Fasten off Spring Green. Weave in ends.
Rnd 2: (RS) With Paddy Green and I hook, attach yarn to where you fastened off, 1sc in same st as joining, 1sc in next 72sc, skip next sc, 1sc in next 8sc, skip next sc, 1sc in next 23sc. Slst to join.
Rnd 3: (RS) Ch1, 1sc in same st as joining, 1sc in next 72sc, skip next sc, 1sc in next 6sc, skip next sc, 1sc in next

Step 1: Working in-between half double crochets.

23sc. Slst to join.

Rnd 4: (RS) Ch1, 1sc in same st as joining, 1sc in next 72sc, skip next sc, 1sc in next 4sc, skip next sc, 1sc in next 23sc. Slst to join. Fasten off and weave in ends.

MIDDLE PIECE UNDER THE PEAS

Row 1: With Paddy Green and I hook, ch7, 1sc in second ch from hook, 1sc in each rem ch. Turn. (6sc)

Row 2: Ch1, 2sc in next sc, 1sc in next 4sc, 2sc in next sc. Turn. (8sc)

Row 3: Ch1, 2sc in next sc, 1sc in next 6sc, 2sc in next sc. Turn. (10sc)

Row 4: Ch1, 2sc in next sc, 1sc in next 8sc, 2sc in next sc. Turn. (12sc)

Rows 5–23: Ch1, 1sc in each sc across. Turn. (12sc)

At end of row 23, fasten off, leaving a long tail to sew with. Put aside for now.

PEAS – MAKE 2

Rnd 1: With I hook and Spring Green, ch2, 6sc in second ch from hook. 6sc) Work in continuous rnds.

Rnd 2: 2sc in each sc around. (12sc)

Rnd 3: 2sc in each sc around. (24sc)

Rnd 4: *1sc in each of the next 3sc, 2sc in the next sc* rep from * to * around. (30sc)

Rnd 5: 1sc in each sc around. (30sc)

Rnd 6: *1sc in next sc, sc next 2sc tog*, rep from * to * until you have about 6sc left. Fasten off Spring Green, leaving a long tail to sew pea to front of cocoon. Stuff pea with polyester fiberfil.

Embroider eyes onto front of pea with Paddy Green yarn.

Embroider mouth with Cherry Red yarn. Sew 1st pea to rows 6 thru 10 on front middle piece, sew 2nd pea to rows 16 thru 20.

Turn cocoon inside out, place middle piece on the trim rows. Sew the middle piece onto the trim on rnd 3 of trim.

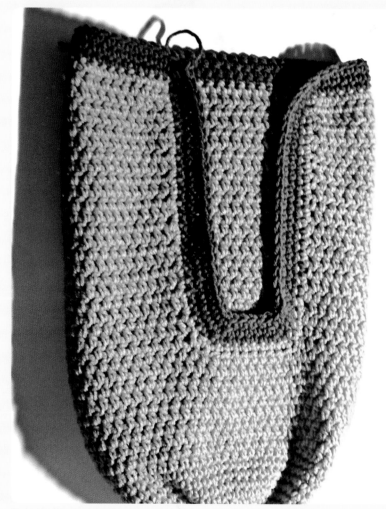

Step 2: Cocoon before panel.

Step 3: Stuff pea.

BEANIE STEM

Rnd 1: (RS) With I hook and Paddy Green, ch2, 5sc in second ch from hook. (5sc) continue in a spiral fashion, using a placemarker if desired.
Rnds 2–4: 1sc in each sc around. (5sc) Fasten off Paddy Green.

BEANIE

NOTE: ch3 counts as first dc.
Rnd 1: With Spring Green and I hook, 2sc in each sc around. Slst to join. (10sc)
Rnd 2: Ch3, 1dc in same st as joining, 2dc in each dc around. Slst to join. (20dc)
Rnd 3: Ch3, 1dc in same st as joining. 1dc in next dc, *2dc in next dc, 1dc in next dc* repeat from * to * around. Slst to join. (30dc)
Rnd 4: Ch3, 1dc in the same st as joining, 1dc in each of the next 2dc, *2dc in the next dc, 1dc in each of the next 2dc* repeat from * to * around. Slst to join. (40dc)
Rnds 5–7: Ch3, 1dc in each dc around. Slst to join. (40dc)
Rnd 8: Ch3, 1dc in each of the next 7dc, dec next 2dc tog, *1dc in each of the next 8dc, dec next 2dc tog* repeat from * to * around. Slst to join. (36dc)

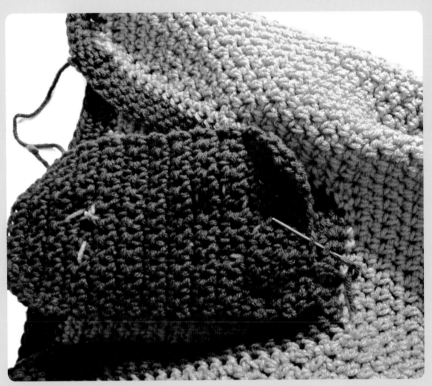
Step 4: Tack in center panel.

Step 5: Slst on top of trc to make point on leaf.

Step 6: Vines and leaves.

Fasten off Spring Green.
Rnd 9: With I hook and Paddy Green, attach yarn to where you fastened off, 1sc in same st as joining, 1sc in each sc around. Slst to join. (36sc)
Rnds 10–11: Ch1, 1sc in same st as joining, 1sc in each sc around. Slst to join. (36sc) Fasten off and weave in ends.

PADDY GREEN LEAVES AND SQUIGGLES

Rnd 1: With I hook and Paddy Green, ch12, slst to first ch to form a circle. Ch1, 1sc in same st as joining, 1sc in each of the remaining 11ch. Slst to join. (12sc)
Rnd 2: Ch1, 1sc in same st as joining, ch12, 2sc in second ch from hook, 2sc in next 10ch, slst in same sc on rnd1, ch12, sc in second ch from hook, 2sc in next 10ch, 1sc in next 3sc, work all of the following in the next sc, (1sc, 1hdc, 1dc, 1trc, ch2, slst in top of trc, 1trc, 1dc, 1hdc, 1sc,) 1slst in next sc, repeat in parenthesis for second leaf, 1slst in next sc, 1sc in next 4sc. Slst to join. Fasten off leaving a tail to sew with. Place hole over stem on hat and tack down the circle and leaves if desired.

Step 7: Attach vines to top of hat.

Flower Bird Nest Cocoon and Diaper Cover

0-2 months

The unique style and bright colors of this adorable nest cocoon and diaper cover are sure to be a hit. Made with 100% soft Peruvian wool, your baby will love snuggling into this fun cocoon.

Materials

- Red Heart Stitch Nation by Debbie Stoller Full O'Sheep 3.5oz/100g/155yds/142m/ # 4medium weight 100% Peruvian wool
  - Color number 2550 / color name Plummy / 2 skeins
  - Color number 2585 / color name French Lavender / 1 skein
  - Color number 2925 / color name Passion Fruit / 1 skein
  - Color number 2630 / color name Meadow / 1 skein
- Yarn Needle
- Scissors

- **Hooks:** US H (8/5.00mm), US K (10.5/6.50mm) and US N (15/10.00mm)

Gauge:
N hook: 7dc – 4",
5dc rows – 4.5"

Skill level: Intermediate

Glossary of abbreviations

beg – beginning
ch – chain
dc – double crochet
dc tog – double crochet together
hdc – half double crochet
rem – remaining
rep – repeat
rnd(s) – round(s)sc – single crochet
slst – slip stitch
st – stitch

NOTE: ch2 counts as first dc for nest
Ch3 counts as first dc for diaper cover

0-2 months = Nest measures approximately 8" tall x 17" long
Diaper cover measures approximately 8.5" circumference x 8" long

BIRD NEST COCOON

Rnd 1: With N hook and 2 strands of Plummy held together, ch23, 2sc in second ch from hook, 1sc in each of the next 20chs, in last ch make 3sc. Now working on the opposite side of ch, 1sc in each of the next 20ch, 1sc in same ch as beg ch. Slst to join. (46sc)

Rnd 2: Ch2, 1dc in same st as joining, 2dc next sc, 1dc in each of the next 20sc, 2dc in each of the next 3sc, 1dc in next 20sc, 2dc in the last sc. Slst to join. (52dc)

Rnd 3: Ch2, 1dc in same st as joining, 2dc in next dc, 1dc in next 24dc, 2dc in next 3dc, 1dc in next 22dc, 2dc in last dc. Slst to join. (58dc)

Rnds 4–9: Ch2, 1dc in each dc around. Slst to join. Ch2 (58dc), at end of rnd 9 fasten off and tie in ends.

LOOPY CUFF TRIM

Rnd 1: With K hook and French Lavender, attach yarn to where you fastened off, with outside of bag facing you, 1sc in each dc around. Slst to join, ch1, turn.

Rnd 2: 1sc in backloop of same st as joining, ch10, 1sc in same backloop, ch10, 1sc in same backloop, 1sc in next backloop, *ch10, 1sc in same

Step 1: Working in-between half double crochets.

Step 2: Ch10 to make loops for cuff trim.

backloop, ch10, 1sc in same backloop, 1sc in next backloop * rep from * to * around. Slst to beg to join. Fasten off and weave in ends.

ROSE FOR TRIM ON NEST

With H hook and Passion Fruit, ch10, 2sc in second ch from hook, 2sc in next 2ch, 2hdc in next 3ch, 2dc in next 3ch. Fasten off leaving a tail to sew with. Roll stitches in a rose and put a stitch thru bottom of rose to hold rolls together. Make as many as desired and sew onto bird nest in desired places.

LEAF FOR TRIM ON NEST

With H hook and Meadow, ch6, 1sc in second ch from hook, 1hdc in next ch, 1dc in next ch, 1hdc in next ch, 3sc in next ch. Now working on opposite side of ch, 1hdc in next ch, 1dc in next ch, 1hdc in next ch, 1slst to first st to join. Fasten off leaving a tail to sew with. Add leaves to nest near each rose or sew leaf under each rose as desired.

Diaper Cover
0–2 months size

Row 1: With H hook and Plummy, ch49, sc in second ch from hook, sc in rem chs. Turn. (48sc)
Row 2: Ch2, dc in first sc and in each sc across row. Turn. (48dc)
Row 3: Ch1, slst across first 16dc, ch2, 1dc in each of the next 17dc, leave the rest of the row unworked. Turn. (18dc)
Row 4: Ch2, dc in first dc, 2dc in next dc, 1dc in each dc across row to last 3 dc, 2dc in next dc, 1dc in next dc, 1dc in turning ch. Turn. (20dc)
Row 5: Ch2, 1dc in each dc across row. Turn. (20dc)
Row 6: Repeat row 4. (22dc)
Row 7: Repeat row 5. (22dc)
Row 8: Repeat row 4. (24dc)
Rows 9–10: Repeat row 5. (24dc)
Row 11: Ch2, 1dc in first dc, dec next two dc together, 1dc in each dc across

Step 3: Working on the opposite side of leaf.

Step 4: Roll the flower in.

Step 5: Tack the flower to hold it together.

Step 6: Sew flower and leaf to loopy cuff trim on both nest and diaper cover.

Step 7: Sew buttons onto diaper cover.

to last 4dc, dec next two dc together, 1dc in next dc, 1dc in turning chain. Turn. (22dc)

Rows 12–14: Repeat row 11. At end of row 14 you will have (16dc)

Rows 15–18: Ch2, 1dc in each dc across rows. Turn. (16dc)

At the end of rnd 18 do not fasten off but continue on to trim.

TRIM

Rnd 1: 1sc in each end of row and st around entire diaper cover. Slst to join. Fasten off and weave in ends.

Rnd 2: With H hook and French Lavender, attach yarn to where you fastened off, 1sc in same st as joining, 1sc in each sc until you reach the top of the button band, *ch6, 1sc in next sc, * rep from * to * across top of button band, then 1sc in each sc back to beg st, slst to join. Fasten off and weave in ends.

Finishing: attach button to front belt where desired.

ROSE FOR WAIST ON DIAPER COVER

With H hook and Passion Fruit, ch7, 2sc in second ch from hook, 2sc in next ch, 2hdc in next 2ch, 2dc in next 2ch. Fasten off leaving a tail to sew with. Roll stitches in a rose and put a stitch thru bottom of rose to hold rolls together. Make as many as desired and sew onto bird nest in desired places.

LEAF FOR WAIST ON DIAPER COVER

With H hook and Meadow, ch5, 1sc in second ch from hook, 1hdc in next 2ch, 3sc in next ch. Now working on opposite side of ch: 1hdc in next 2ch, 1sc last ch, 1slst to first st to join. Fasten off leaving a tail to sew with. Sew leaf under each rose as desired. Attach roses and leaves to waistband on diaper cover.

Snowflake Bird Nest Cocoon and Diaper Cover

0-2 months

Let your little one snuggle up in this adorable snowflake bird nest and diaper cover! Double strands of a nice soft yarn and a large hook size help to make this a quick and easy cocoon to make.

Materials

- Bernat Baby Coordinates 5oz/140g/457yds/418m #3 light weight 71.2% acrylic, 25.6%rayon, 3.2%nylon
- Bernat Softee Baby 5oz/140g/362yds/331m #3 light weight 100% acrylic
- Color number 02000 / color name White / 1 skein
- Lion Brand Fun Fur 1.75oz/50g/64yds/58m #5 bulky weight 100% polyester
- Color number 100 / color name White / 2 skeins
- 1" wide white satin ribbon, 2 yards
- Yarn Needle
- Scissors

- **Hook:** US K (10.5/6.50mm)

Gauge:
K hook: 3" x 3" – 8sc x 8sc rows

Skill level: Intermediate

Glossary of abbreviations

beg – beginning
ch – chain
ch3sp – chain 3 spacesc – single crochet
dc – double crochet
rep – repeat
rnd(s) – round(s)
sk – skip
slst – slip stitch
st – stitch
tog – together

NOTE: ch3 counts as first dc

0-2 months = Nest measures approximately 9" tall x 16" long
Diaper cover measures approximately 8.5" circumference x 8" long

BIRD NEST COCOON

Rnd 1: With K hook and one strand of White Baby Coordinates and one strand of Softee Baby held tog, ch33, 2sc in second ch from hook, 1sc in next 30ch, 3sc in last ch. Now working on opposite side of ch, 1sc in next 30ch, 1sc in same ch as beg sc. Slst to join. (66sc)

Rnd 2: Ch1, 2sc in same st as joining, 2sc in next sc, 1sc in next 30sc, 2sc in next 3sc, 1sc in next 30sc, 2sc in last sc. Slst to join. (72sc)

Rnd 3: Ch1, 2sc in same st as joining, 1sc in next sc, 2sc in next sc, 1sc in next 31sc, (2sc in next sc, 1sc in next sc) rep 2 more times, 1sc in next 30sc, 2sc in next sc, 1sc in last sc. Slst to join. (78sc)

Rnd 4: Ch1, 2sc in same st as joining, 1sc in next 2sc, 2sc in next sc, 1sc in next 34sc, (2sc in next sc, 1sc in next 2sc) rep 2 more times, 1sc in next 28sc, 2sc in next sc, 1sc in last 2sc. Slst to join. (84sc)

Rnd 5: Ch1, 2sc in same st as joining, 1sc in next 3sc, 2sc in next sc, 1sc in

Step 1: Working on back side of chain.

Step 2: Pattern for rnd 7.

next 35sc, (2sc in next sc, 1sc in next 3sc) rep 2 more times, 1sc in next 28sc, 2sc in next sc, 1sc in last 3sc. Slst to join. (90sc)

Rnd 6: Ch1, 1sc in each sc around. Slst to join. (90sc)

Rnd 7: Ch1, (1sc, ch3, 1sc) all in same st as joining,* sk next 3sc, (2dc, ch3, 2dc) all in next sc, sk next 3sc, (1sc, ch3, 1sc) all in next sc*. Rep from * to * 9 more times, sk next 4sc, (2dc, ch3, 2dc) all in next sc, sk next 4sc. Slst to in first sc to join. Slst into next ch3sp,

Rnd 8: Ch3, 1dc, ch3, 2dc all in same ch sp as joining, (1sc, ch3, 1sc) all in next ch3sp, * (2dc, ch3, 2dc) all in next ch3sp, (1sc, ch3, 1sc) all in next ch3sp*. Rep from * to * around. Slst to top of ch3 to join. Slst into next ch3sp.

Rnd 9: Ch1, (1sc, ch3, 1sc) all in same st as joining, (2dc, ch3, 2dc) all in next ch3sp, *(1sc, ch3, 1sc) all in next ch3sp, (2dc, ch3, 2dc) all in next ch3sp*. Rep from * to *. Slst to in first sc to join. Slst into next ch3sp.

Rnds 10–16: Repeat rnds 8 and 9 alternately.

Rnd 17: Slst into first ch3sp, ch1, 1sc in same st as joining, 1sc in each sc and in each dc around and work only 1sc in each ch3 loop. Slst to join. Fasten off and weave in ends. (88sc)

FLUFFY WHITE TRIM

Rnd 1: With K hook and 2 strands of White Fun Fur held tog, attach yarn to front loop on any sc, ch2, 1dc in front loops of each sc around. Slst to join. (88dc)

Rnd 2: Ch3, 1dc in both loops of each dc around. Slst to join. Fasten off and weave in ends. Fold rnds 1 and 2 down.

DIAPER COVER

Rnd 1: With K hook and one strand of Baby Coordinates and one strand of Softee Baby held tog, ch2, 6sc in second ch from hook. (6sc) Slst to join.

Rnds 2–3: Ch1, 2sc in same st as

joining, 2sc in each sc around. Slst to join. (24sc)

Rnd 4: Ch1, 1sc in same st as joining, 2sc in next sc, *1sc in next sc, 2sc in next sc*. Rep from * to * around. Slst to join. (36sc)

Rnd 5: Ch1, 1sc in same st as joining, 1sc in next sc,(first leg opening) ch18, skip next 15sc, 1sc in next 3sc, (second leg opening) ch18, skip next 15sc, 1sc in last sc. Slst to join.

Rnd 6: Ch1, 1sc in same st as joining, 1sc in next sc, 1sc in next 18ch, 1sc in next 3sc, 1sc in next 18ch, 1sc in next sc. Slst to join. (42sc)

Rnd 7: Ch1, (1sc, ch3, 1sc) all in same st as joining, sk next 2sc, (2dc, ch3, 2dc) all in next sc, *sk next 2sc, (1sc, ch3, 1sc) all in next sc, sk next 2sc, (2dc, ch3, 2dc) all in next sc*. Rep from * to *. Slst in first sc to join. Slst into next ch3sp.

Rnd 8: Ch3, 1dc, ch3, 2dc all in same ch sp as joining, (1sc, ch3, 1sc) all in next ch3sp, *(2dc, ch3, 2dc) all in next ch3sp, (1sc, ch3, 1sc) all in next ch3 sp*. Rep from * to * around. Slst to top of ch3 to join. Slst into next ch3sp.

Rnd 9: Ch1, (1sc, ch3, 1sc) all in same st as joining, (2dc, ch3, 2dc) all in next ch3sp, *(1sc, ch3, 1sc) all in next ch3sp, (2dc, ch3, 2dc) all in next ch3sp*. Rep from * to *. Slst in first sc to join. Slst into next ch3sp.

Rnd 10: Repeat rnd 8.

Rnd 11: Repeat rnd 9.

Rnd 12: Slst into first ch3sp, ch1, 1sc in same st as joining, skip next sc, *1sc in next dc, skip next dc, 1sc in next ch3sp, skip next dc, 1sc in next dc, skip next sc, 1sc in next ch3sp, skip next sc*. Rep from * to * around. Slst to join. (28sc)

Rnd 13: Ch3, 1dc in each sc around. Slst to top of ch3. Ch1 (28dc)

Rnd 14: 1sc in same st as joining, 1sc in

Step 3: Working pattern in rnd 8.

Step 4: Adding fur trim.

Step 5: Fold down trim.

Step 6: Adding trim to leg openings.

each dc around. Slst to join. Fasten off and weave in ends.

LEG HOLE OPENINGS
Rnd 1: With K hook and one strand of Baby Coordinates and one strand of Softee Baby held tog, attach yarns to any st in leg opening. 1sc in same st as joining, 1sc in each st around each leg opening. Slst to join. (36sc) Fasten off and weave in ends.

FLUFFY TRIM ON LEG OPENINGS
Rnd 1: With K hook and two strands of White Fun Fur held tog, attach yarn to any sc. 1sc in each sc around each leg opening. Slst to join. (36sc) Fasten off and weave in ends.

FLUFFY TRIM ON WAIST
Rnd 1: With K hook and two strands of White Fun Fur held tog, attach yarn to any sc, 1sc in each sc around. Slst to join. (28sc) Fasten off and weave in ends.
Finishing: Tie a bow on one side of nest through any stitches on side. Weave satin ribbon around waist of diaper cover through rnd 13 of diaper cover. Tie bow in front of diaper cover.

Step 7: Weave ribbon through nest and diaper cover.

Afghans

Dragonfly Baby Afghan

Baby Pram Afghan

Dragonfly Baby Afghan

This sweet dragonfly afghan is sure to keep your little ones snug and warm.

Materials

- Berroco Ultra Alpaca 3.5oz/100g/215yds/198m Worsted weight 50% Alpaca, 50% wool
- Color number 6214 / color name Steel Cut Oats / 2 skeins
- Color number 6221 / color name Deep Purple / 2 skeins
- Color number 6233 / color name Rose Spice / 2 skeins
- Color number 6235 / color name Fuchsia / 2 skeins
- Yarn needle
- Scissors

- **Hooks:** US F (5/3.75mm) and US G (6/4.00mm)

Skill level: Advanced

Gauge:
F hook: 17sc – 4.25",
21sc rows – 4"

Glossary of abbreviations

7hdc cluster – 7half double crochet cluster – yo, insert hook into next sc, bring yarn back through, (yarn over, insert hook in same sc, bring yarn back through) repeat 5 more times, keeping all 15 loops on hook, yo, drop off all 15 loops on hook.

ch – chain

dc – double crochet

fpdc – front post double crochet

hdc – half double crochet

rnd(s) – round(s)

RS – right side of work

sc – single crochet

slst – slip stitch

st – stitch

yo – yarn over

You are going to make 6 strips; follow the sequence instructions for each strip. Make sure to start all next colors on right side of work.
Each strip will have a beginning plain block or a beginning dragonfly block. See instructions below on how to start each strip. See instructions below also for each strip sequence.

TO MAKE BEGINNING DRAGONFLY BLOCK

Row 1: (beginning dragonfly blocks) With G hook, ch16, 1sc in second ch from hook, 1sc in next 14ch. Turn. (15sc)

Row 2: Ch1, 1sc in each sc across. Turn. (15sc)

Row 3: Ch1, 1sc in next 7sc, 1dc in next sc, 1sc in next 7sc. Turn. (15sts)

Row 4: Ch1, 1sc in next 15sts. Turn. (15sc)

Row 5: Ch1, 1sc in next 7sc, 1fpdc around dc, 1sc in next 7sc. Turn. (15sts)

Row 6: Ch1, 1sc in next 15sts. Turn. (15sc)

Row 7: Ch1, 1sc in next 7sc, 1fpdc around fpdc, 1sc in next 7sc. Turn. (15sts)

Row 8: Ch1, 1sc in next 15sts. Turn. (15sc)

Row 9: Ch1, 1sc in next 7sc, 1fpdc around fpdc, 1sc in next 7sc. Turn. (15sts)

Row 10: Ch1, 1sc in next 7sc, 1slst in next st, (wing) ch12, 1slst in next same st, (wing) ch12, 1slst in same st, 1sc in next 7sc. Turn. (15sts)

Row 11: Ch1, 1sc in next 3sc, *hold ch12 in front of next sc, insert hook thru end of wing and then into next sc, pull yarn back thru and yo and drop off 2loops, * 1sc in next 3sc behind the wing, push wing back, 1fpdc around fpdc, push wing forward, skip next 2slst, 1sc in next 3sc, repeat from * to * to secure second wing down, 1sc in next 3sc. Turn.

Row 12: Ch1, 1sc in next 7sc, 1slst in next st, (wing) ch12, 1slst in same st, (wing) ch12, 1slst in same st, 1sc in

next 7sc. Turn. (15sts)

Row 13: Repeat row 11

Row 14: Ch1, 1sc in next 7sc, (form head) 7hdc cluster in next st, 1sc in next 7sc. Turn.

Row 15: Ch1, 1sc in next 7sc, 1sc in top of cluster, 1sc in next 7sc. Turn. (15sts)

Rows 16–17: Ch1, 1sc in next 15sts, turn. At end of row 17 fasten off.

STEEL CUT OATS EDGING

Row 1: With G hook and Steel Cut Oats, attach yarn to RS of work, 1sc in same st as joining, 1sc in next 14sc. Turn. (15sc)

Rows 2–3: Ch1, 1sc in each sc across. Turn. (15sc) end of row 3 fasten off. Work rows 1–3 in between each block.

TO MAKE PLAIN BLOCKS

Row 1: With G hook and color needed, attach yarn to RS of work, to first sc on last row of Steel Cut Oats, 1sc in same st as joining. Turn. (15sc)

Rows 2–17: Ch1, 1sc in each sc across. Turn. (15sc) At end of row 17 fasten off.

DRAGONFLY BLOCK

Row 1: (dragonfly square) With G hook, attach yarn to right side of work, 1sc in same st as joining, 1sc in each sc across. Turn. (15sc)

Row 2: Ch1, 1sc in each sc across. Turn. (15sc)

Row 3: Ch1, 1sc in next 7sc, 1dc in next sc, 1sc in next 7sc. Turn. (15sts)

Row 4: Ch1, 1sc in next 15sts. Turn. (15sc)

Row 5: Ch1, 1sc in next 7sc, 1fpdc around dc, 1sc in next 7sc. Turn. (15sts)

Row 6: Ch1, 1sc in next 15sts. Turn. (15sc)

Row 7: Ch1, 1sc in next 7sc, 1fpdc around fpdc, 1sc in next 7sc. Turn. (15sts)

Row 8: Ch1, 1sc in next 15sts. Turn. (15sc)

Row 9: Ch1, 1sc in next 7sc, 1fpdc around fpdc, 1sc in next 7sc. Turn. (15sts)

Step 1: Fpdc around fpdc from prev row.

Step 2: 2 sets of ch12 to form 2 wings.

Row 10: Ch1, 1sc in next 7sc, 1slst in next st, (wing) ch12, 1slst in next same st, (wing) ch12, 1slst in same st, 1sc in next 7sc. Turn. (15sts)

Row 11: Ch1, 1sc in next 3sc, *hold ch12 in front of next sc, insert hook thru end of wing and then into next sc, pull yarn back thru and yo and drop off 2loops* 1sc in next 3sc behind the wing, push wing back, 1fpdc around fpdc, push wing forward, skip next 2slst, 1sc in next 3sc, repeat from * to * to secure second wing down, 1sc in next 3sc. Turn.

Row 12: Ch1, 1sc in next 7sc, 1slst in next st, (wing) ch12, 1slst in same st, (wing) ch12, 1slst in same st, 1sc in next 7sc. Turn. (15sts)

Row 13: Repeat row 11

Row 14: Ch1, 1sc in next 7sc, (form head) 7hdc cluster in next st, 1sc in next 7sc. Turn.

Row 15: Ch1, 1sc in next 7sc, 1sc in top of cluster, 1sc in next 7sc. Turn. (15sts)

Rows 16–17: Ch1, 1sc in next 15sts, turn. At end of row 17 fasten off.

TO MAKE PLAIN BLOCKS

Row 1: With G hook and color needed, attach yarn to RS of work, to first sc on last row of Steel Cut Oats, 1sc in same st as joining. Turn. (15sc)

Rows 2–17: Ch1, 1sc in each sc across. Turn. (15sc) At end of row 17 fasten off.

1ST STRIP SEQUENCE

1st block – Fuchsia, make beginning dragonfly block

Work next 3 rows in sc in Steel Cut Oats.

second block – Rose Spice, make plain block.

Work next 3 rows in sc in Steel Cut Oats.

3rd block – Deep Purple, make dragonfly block.

Work next 3 rows in sc in Steel Cut Oats.

4th block – Fuchsia, make plain block.

Work next 3 rows in sc in Steel Cut

Step 3: Sc thru wing and sc under wing.

Step 4: Fpdc around fpdc from prev rnd.

Step 5: 7hdc cluster for head.

Step 6: Yarn over and drop off all loops on hook to form head.

Oats.

5th block – Rose Spice, make dragonfly block.

Work next 3 rows in sc Steel Cut Oats.

6th block – Deep Purple, make plain block.

2ND STRIP SEQUENCE

1st block – Rose Spice, make beginning plain block.

Work next 3 rows in sc in Steel Cut Oats.

2nd block – Deep Purple, make dragonfly block.

Work next 3 rows in sc in Steel Cut Oats.

3rd block – Fuchsia, make plain block.

Work next 3 rows in sc in Steel Cut Oats.

4th block – Rose Spice, make dragonfly block.

Work next 3 rows in sc Steel Cut Oats.

5th block – Deep Purple, make plain block.

Work next 3 rows in sc with Steel Cut Oats.

6th block – Fuchsia, make dragonfly block.

3RD STRIP SEQUENCE

1st block – Deep Purple, make beginning dragonfly block.

Work next 3 rows in sc in Steel Cut Oats.

2nd block – Fuchsia, make plain block.

Work next 3 rows in sc in Steel Cut Oats.

3rd block – Rose Spice, make dragonfly block.

Work next 3 rows in sc Steel Cut Oats.

4th block – Deep Purple, make plain block.

Work next 3 rows in sc with Steel Cut Oats.

5th block – Fuchsia, make dragonfly block.

Work next 3 rows in sc with Steel Cut Oats.

6th block – Rose Spice, make plain block.

4TH STRIP SEQUENCE

1st block – Fuchsia, make beginning plain block.

Work next 3 rows in sc in Steel Cut Oats.

2nd block – Rose Spice, make dragonfly block.

Work next 3 rows in sc Steel Cut Oats.

3rd block – Deep Purple, make plain block.

Work next 3 rows in sc with Steel Cut Oats.

4th block – Fuchsia, make dragonfly block.

Work next 3 rows in sc with Steel Cut Oats.

5th block – Rose Spice, make plain block.

Work next 3 rows in sc with Steel Cut Oats.

6th block – Deep Purple, make dragonfly block.

5TH STRIP SEQUENCE

1st block – Rose Spice, make beginning dragonfly block.

Work next 3 rows in sc Steel Cut Oats.

2nd block – Deep Purple, make plain block.

Work next 3 rows in sc with Steel Cut Oats.

3rd block – Fuchsia, make dragonfly block.

Work next 3 rows in sc with Steel Cut Oats.

4th block – Rose Spice, make plain block.

Work next 3 rows in sc with Steel Cut Oats.

5th block – Deep Purple, make dragonfly block.

Work next 3 rows in sc with Steel Cut Oats.

6th block – Fuchsia, make plain block.

6TH STRIP SEQUENCE

1st block – Deep Purple, make beginning plain block.

Work next 3 rows in sc with Steel Cut Oats.

Step 7: 1sc in top of head.

Step 8: 3 rows of Steel Cut Oats in between each square.

2nd block – Fuchsia, make dragonfly block.
Work next 3 rows in sc with Steel Cut Oats.
3rd block – Rose Spice, make plain block.
Work next 3 rows in sc with Steel Cut Oats.
54th block – Deep Purple, make dragonfly block.
Work next 3 rows in sc with Steel Cut Oats.
5th block – Fuchsia, make plain block.
Work next 3 rows in sc with Steel Cut Oats.
6th block– Rose Spice, make dragonfly block.

VERTICAL BORDERS

NOTE: after all strips are made work 2 rows of borders along both vertical sides of each strip. Do not make 2 rows on the first strip on the left side and do not make 2 rows on the last strip on the right side or outside border.

Row 1: With F hook and Steel Cut Oats, attach yarn to right side of work and working in the ends of rows, 1sc in each end of row along entire side of strip. Turn.
Row 2: Ch1, 1sc in each sc across. Fasten off. Repeat rows 1 and 2 for other side of strip.

JOINING STRIPS

With F hook and Steel Cut Oats, and with strips 1 and 2 held tog, the right sides facing each other, sc tog the 2 strips, making sure the horizontal lines match. Fasten off, weave in ends. Repeat same for all strips in order according to sequence. After you finish connecting the last two strips, do not fasten off but continue on outside border.

OUTSIDE BORDER

Rnd 1: With F hook, and Steel Cut Oats, with right side of work facing you, (1sc in next 3sts, skip next st) rep to first corner, work 3sc in first corner, *(1sc in next 3sts or ends of rows, skip next st or end of row) rep to next corner, 3sc in next corner* rep from * to * around, ending with (1sc in next 3sts, skip next st) rep to end of rnd. Slst to join.
Rnds 2–4: Ch1, 1sc in same st as joining, 1sc in each sc and in each corner st, work 3sc. Slst to join. Fasten off and weave in ends.

Step 9: 2 rows of Steel Cut Oats in sides of strips.

Baby Pram Afghan

This warm wool pram blanket is bright and stylish. Use a large hook to make this blanket in a jiffy.

Materials

- Cascade Yarns Greenland 3.5oz/100g/137yds/125m 100% Merino superwash
  – Color number 3530 / color name Burnt Orange / 8 balls
  – Color number 3518 / color name Blue Hawaii / 2 balls

- **Hook:** US K (10.5/6.50mm)

Skill level: Intermediate

Gauge:
1 cluster row – 1", 4 clusters – 2"

Glossary of abbreviations

Beg corner cluster – Ch3, yo, insert hook into corner ch sp, bring yarn back through, yo, drop off first 2 loops, yo, insert hook in same ch sp, bring yarn back through, yo, drop off first 2 loops, yo, drop off all three loops, ch2, 3dc cluster in same corner ch sp.

ch – chain

Cluster – yo, insert hook into ch1sp, pull yarn back thru, yo, drop off first 2 loops, yo, insert hook into same ch1sp, bring yarn back thru, yo, drop off first 2 loops, yo, insert hook into same ch1sp, bring yarn back thru, yo, drop off first 2loops, yo, drop off all 4loops on hook.

Corner Cluster – cluster, ch2, cluster

dc – double crochet

rep – repeat

rnd(s) – round(s)

RS – right side

sc – single crochet

sk – skip

sp – space

yo – yarn over hook

NOTE: ch3 counts as first dc
Finished size = 36" x 40"

BLANKET

Row 1: With K hook and Burnt Orange, ch 90, 1sc in second ch from hook,* ch1, sk next ch, 1sc in next ch* rep from * to * across. Turn.

Row 2: Ch3, cluster in next ch1 sp, *ch1, skip next sc, cluster in next ch1sp* rep from * to * across to last sc, 1dc in last sc. Turn.

Row 3: Ch1, 1sc in top of dc, ch1, *sk next cluster, 1sc in next ch1sp, ch1* rep from * to * across to last st, 1sc in top of ch3. Turn.

Row 4: Ch1, 1sc in first sc, 1sc in next ch1sp, *ch1, sk next sc, 1sc in next ch1sp* rep from * to * across, 1sc in last sc. Turn.

Row 5: Ch1, 1sc in first sc, *ch1, sk next sc, 1sc in next ch1sp* rep from * to * across, 1sc in last sc. Turn.

Row 6: Repeat row 4.

Row 7: Repeat row 5.

Rows 8–73: Repeat rows 2–7 in sequence for pattern.

Row 74: Repeat row 2.

Row 75: Repeat row 3. Do not fasten off but continue on to border.

BORDER

Rnd 1: Working around the next 3 sides of afghan, Ch2, 1sc in same st as ending st on row 74, ch1, *sk next end of row, 1sc in next end of row, ch1* rep from * to * across to next corner, (1sc, ch2, 1sc) in corner, ch1, *sk next st, 1sc in next st, ch1* rep from * to * across to next corner, (1sc, ch2, 1sc) in corner, ch1, *sk next end of row, 1sc in next end of row, ch1* rep from * to * across to next corner, (1sc, ch2, 1sc) in last corner. Slst to join, fasten off, weave in ends.

Rnd 2: With Blue Hawaii and K hook, attach yarn to RS of any ch2 corner st. Beg corner cluster in same corner ch sp, *ch1, skip next sc, cluster in next ch1sp* rep from * to * across to corner ch sp, work corner cluster, repeat from * to * across to next corner ch sp, work corner cluster, repeat from * to * across to next corner ch sp, corner cluster, repeat from * to * across. Ch1, slst to join, turn.

Rnd 3: Ch1, 1sc in first ch1 sp, ch1, *sk next cluster, 1sc in next ch1sp, ch1* repeat from * to * across to corner ch

Step 1: 1st step to make a cluster.

Step 2: 2nd step in making a cluster.

Step 3: 3rd step in making a cluster.

sp, (1sc, ch2, 1sc) all in corner ch sp, repeat from *to * across to corner ch sp, (1sc, ch2, 1sc) all in corner ch sp, repeat from * to * across to corner ch sp, (1sc, ch2, 1sc) all in corner ch sp, repeat from * to * across to corner ch sp, (1sc, ch2, 1sc) all in corner ch sp, ch1, slst to join, fasten off, weave in ends.

Rnds 4–5: With Burnt Orange and K hook, repeat rows 2–3. At end of row 5, fasten off, weave in ends.

Rnds 6–7: With Blue Hawaii and K hook, repeat rows 2–3. At end of row 7, fasten off, weave in ends.

Rnds 8–11: With Burnt Orange and k hook, repeat rows 2–3. At end of row 11, fasten off, weave in ends.

Step 4: Drop off all 4 loops to complete cluster.

Step 5: Making a cluster in a corner. Make one cluster, ch1, (start of 2nd cluster) yo, insert hook into same sp, yo, drop off first 2loops.

Step 6: Yo, insert hook in same sp, bring yarn back thru, yo, drop off first 2 loops.

Step 7: Yo, insert hook in same sp, bring yarn back thru, yo, drop off first 2loops.

Step 8: Yo, drop off all 4 loops on hook. One cluster st completed.

Other Crochet Bits

Baby Bib with Sheep Applique

Girl Bootees

Boy Bootees

Legwarmers for Babies
 and Toddlers

Baby Bib with Sheep Applique

Pretty bright cotton baby bibs.

Materials

- Cascade Yarn Cotton Rich 50g/80yds #4 medium weight
  64% cotton/ 36% nylon
- Color number 5186 / color name Jean's Fave (turquoise) /1 skein
- Color number 2194 / color name Sour Apple (green) / 1 skein
- Cascade Yarn Cotton Rich DK 50g/135.60yds
  64%cotton/ 36%nylon
- Color number 8176 / color name Natural – 1 skein
- Color number 8990 / color name Black – 1 skein
- Yarn needle
- Scissors

- **Hooks:** US G (6/4.00mm)
  and US H (8/5.00mm)

Gauge:
G hook: 7sc – 2", 7sc rows – 2"
H hook: 6sc – 2", 6sc rows – 2"

Skill level: Easy

Glossary of abbreviations

ch – chain
dc – double crochet
rem – remaining
rnd(s) – round(s)
sc – single crochet
slst – slip stitch
sts – stitches
tog – together

Use G hook to make 0–12months size bib – 6" wide x 5.5" tall
Use H hook to make 18–24months size bib – 7" wide x 6" tall
Use G hook to make sheep for both sizes

BIB

Row 1: With G or H hook and Sour Apple, ch19, 1sc in second ch from hook, 1dc in next ch, *1sc in next ch, 1dc in next ch* rep from * to * across. Turn. (18sts)

Rows 2–5: Ch1, *1sc in next dc, 1dc in next sc* rep from * to * across. Turn. (18sts)

At end of row 5 fasten off Sour Apple.

Row 6: With G or H hook and Jean's Fave (turquoise), attach yarn to right side of work, 1sc in same st as joining, 1sc in next 17sts. Turn. (18sc)

Rows 7–15: Ch1, 1sc in each sc across.

Turn. (18sc)

Neck Rows and Ties

Row 1: Ch1, 1sc in next 4sc. Turn (4sc) leaving the rest of the row unworked for now.

Row 2: Ch1, 1sc in next 4sc. Turn. (4sc)

Row 3: Ch1, 1sc in next 2sc, sc tog the last 2sc. Turn. (3sc)

Row 4: Ch1, sc tog the next 2sc, 1sc in next sc. Turn. (2sc)

Row 5: Ch1, sc tog the next 2sc. Turn.

Next: working across the neck edge of bib. Ch1, 1slst in each end of row, 1sc in next 14sc on neck edge. Turn.

Row 1: Ch1, 1sc in next 4sc. Turn. (4sc)

Row 2: Ch1, sc tog the first 2sc, 1sc in next 2sc. Turn. (3sc)

Row 3: Ch1, 1sc in next sc, sc tog the next 2sc. Turn. (2sc)

Row 4: Ch1, sc tog the next 2sc. (1sc)

Do not fasten off, but continue on to first tie.

First tie: Ch40, 1slst in second ch from hook, 1slst in each rem ch. Do not fasten off but continue on to trim.

Trim

Rnd 1: 1sc in each end of row to first corner, 2sc in corner, 1sc in each st

Step 1: Sc in the dc.

Step 2: Dc in the sc.

on opposite side of starting ch, 2sc in corner, 1sc in each end of row up to tip, (second tie) ch40, 1slst in second ch from hook, 1slst in each rem ch, slst in same st to join. Fasten off and weave in ends.

SHEEP

Rnd 1: With G hook and Natural, ch2, 6sc in second ch from hook. Slst to join. (6sc)

Rnd 2: Ch1, 2sc in same st as joining, 2sc in each sc around. Slst to join. (12sc)

Rnd 3: Ch1, 2sc in same st as joining, 2sc in each sc around. Slst to join. (24sc)

Rnd 4: Ch1, 1sc in same st as joining, 1sc in each sc around. Slst to join. (24sc)

Fasten off Natural leaving a tail to sew with.

Ear and Face

Row 1: With G hook and Black (ear) ch5, 1sc in second ch from hook, 1sc in next 3ch, attach yarn to any sc on sheep body, 1sc in same st as joining, 1sc in next 3sc. Turn. (4sc)

Row 2: Ch1, (sc tog the next 2sc) twice. Turn. (2sc)

Row 3: Sc tog the next 2sc, ch1, slst in next 2 ends of rows on face. Fasten off leaving a tail to sew with.

Feet

With G hook and Black, skip 2sc after face, attach Black to next sc, 3sc in same st as joining, slst in next sc, 3sc in next sc. Fasten off leaving a tail to sew with.

Tail

With G hook and Black, skip next 3sc after feet, attach yarn to next sc, 1slst in same st as joining, ch3, 1slst in second ch from hook, 1slst in next ch, slst in same st as beg. Fasten off leaving a tail to sew with.

Attaching Sheep to Bib

With Natural, sew sheep body onto front of bib. Weave in ends. Then sew the face, feet and tail using the tails you left when you fastened off. Weave in all ends.

Step 3: Make ear and sc in next 4sc.

Step 4: Face and ear made.

Step 5: Feet.

Step 6: Tail.

Step 7: Sew body on first, then sew black parts down.

Girl Bootees

Made with a soft wool/acrylic blend, these bright bootees are easy to make and fun to wear.

Materials

- Plymouth Encore Knitting Worsted 3.5oz/100g/200yds
  #4 medium weight
  75%acrylic, 25%wool
  – Color number 3335/ Color name Lime / 1 skein
  – Color number 0458/Color name Purple Orchid / 1 skein
- Yarn needle
- Scissors

- **Hook:** US G (6/4.00mm)

Gauge:
1" x 1" – 3sc x 3sc rows

Skill level: Easy

Glossary of abbreviations

ch – chain
hdc – half double crochet
rnd(s) – round(s)
sc – single crochet
sk – skip
slst – slip stitch

0-6 months = 5.5" tall, 6" circumference
6-12 months = 6.5" tall, 7" circumference

SOCK BOOTEE – MAKE 2
0–6 months size only
Rnd 1: With G hook and Purple Orchid, ch2, 6sc in second ch from hook. (6sc) Continue in a spiral fashion, using a place marker if desired.
Rnd 2: 2sc in each sc around. (12sc)
Rnd 3: *1sc in next sc, 2sc in next sc* rep from * to * around. (18sc)
Rnd 4: (2sc in next sc, 1sc in next 8sc) rep one more time. (20sc)
Rnds 5–7: 1sc in each sc around. (20sc) do not fasten off Purple Orchid, but change to Lime.
Rnd 8: With Lime, 1sc in each sc around. (20sc) change back to Purple Orchid
Rnd 9: With Purple Orchid, 1sc in each sc around. (20sc) change back to Lime
Rnds 10–21: Repeat rnds 8 and 9 alternately. Ending with Purple Orchid rnd. (20sc) Change back to Lime, fasten off Purple Orchid and weave in ends.
Rnds 22–23: 1sc in each sc around. Slst to join. Turn. (20sc)
Rnd 24: Ch1, 1sc in the back loops of same st as joining, 1sc in the back loops of each sc around. Slst to join. (20sc)
Rnd 25: 1sc in same st as joining, *sk next sc, 6hdc in next sc, sk next sc, 1slst in next sc* rep from *to * around. Slst to join. Fasten off leaving a tail to tack the scallops down with.

SOCK BOOTEE – MAKE 2
6–12 months size only
Rnd 1: With G hook and Purple Orchid, ch2, 6sc in second ch from hook. (6sc) Continue in a spiral fashion, using a place marker if desired.
Rnds 2–3: 2sc in each sc around. (24sc)
Rnds 4–7: 1sc in each sc around. (24sc) do not fasten off Purple Orchid, but change to Lime.
Rnd 8: With Lime, 1sc in each sc around. (24sc) Change back to Purple Orchid.
Rnd 9: With Purple Orchid, 1sc in each sc around. (24sc) Change back to Lime.
Rnds 10–23: Repeat rnds 8 and 9 alternately. Ending with Purple Orchid rnd. (24sc) Change back to Lime, fasten off Purple Orchid and weave in ends.
Rnds 24–25: 1sc in each sc around. Slst to join. Turn. (24sc)
Rnd 26: Ch1, 1sc in the back loops of same st as joining, 1sc in the back loops of each sc around. Slst to join. (24sc)
Rnd 27: 1sc in same st as joining, *sk next sc, 6hdc in next sc, sk next sc, 1slst in next sc* rep from *to * around. Slst to join. Fasten off leaving a tail to tack the scallops down with.

Step 1: Switching colors for stripes.

Step 2: Working in the back loop for cuff.

Step 3: Making ruffles.

Step 4: *Tack down ruffles.*

Boy Bootees

Handsome and warm is this great looking baby bootee. Your little one will be looking very stylish in the newsboy boy bootee. Make with simple single crochets and a front post single crochet.

Materials

- Red Heart Stitch Nation by Debbie Stoller/ Alpaca Love
  3oz/85g/132yds/121m #4 medium weight
  80%wool/20%alpaca
  – Color number 3350 / color name Espresso Bean/ 1 skein
  – Color number 3810 / color name Lake/ 1 skein
- ½" buttons x 4
- Yarn needle
- Scissors
- **Hooks:** US H (8/5.00mm) and US I (9/5.50mm)

Gauge:
H hook: 1" x 1",
3sc x 3sc rows

Skill level: Intermediate

Glossary of abbreviations

ch – chain
dc tog – double crochet together
fpsc – front post single crochet
rnd(s) – round(s)
sc – single crochet
slst – slip stitch
yo – yarn over hook

NOTE: to make a fpsc – front post single crochet – insert hook behind sc, and come back up on other side of same single crochet. Yo, drop off 2 loops on hook.

0–3 months size, 3.5" sole
3–6 months size, 4" sole
6–12 months size, 4.5" sole

SOLE
Rnd 1: With H hook, and Espresso Bean, ch7 (ch9, ch10), 2sc in second ch from hook, 1sc in next 4ch (6ch, 7ch), 5sc in last ch. Working on opposite side of ch, 1sc in next 4ch (6ch, 7ch), 1sc in same ch as beg. Slst to join. (16sc, 20sc, 22sc)
Rnd 2: Ch1, 1sc in same st as joining, 1sc in next 6sc (8sc, 9sc) 2sc in next 3sc, 1sc in next 6sc (8sc, 9sc). Slst to join. (19sc, 23sc, 25sc)
Rnd 3: Ch1, 2sc in same st as joining, 2sc in next sc, 1sc in next 5sc (7sc, 8sc), *2sc in next sc, 1sc in next sc * rep from * to 3 more times. 1Sc in next 3sc (5sc, 6sc) 2sc in the last sc. Slst to join. (26sc, 30sc, 32sc)
Rnd 4: Ch1, 1fpsc around each sc around. Slst to join. Fasten off Espresso Bean. (26fpsc, 30fpsc, 32fpsc)

SIDES
Rnd 1: With H hook and Lake, attach yarn to under the two loops behind the fpsc, near where you fastened off, 1sc in same st as joining, 1sc under the two loops that are behind each fpsc around. Continue in a spiral fashion. (26sc, 30sc, 32sc)
Rnd 2: 1sc in each sc around. (26sc, 30sc, 32sc)
Rnd 3: 1sc in next 9sc (10sc, 10sc), (dc tog the next 2sc) rep 5, (6, 7 more times), 1sc in next 5sc (6sc, 6sc). (20sts, 23sts, 24sts)
Rnd 4: 1sc in next 8sc (9sc, 9sc), *dc tog the next 2dc* rep 3, (4, 4 more times), 1sc in next 4sc(4sc,5sc). (16sts, 18sts, 19sts)
Rnd 5: 1sc in each st around. (16sc, 18sc, 19sc)
Rnds 6–12: 1sc in each sc around. (16sc, 18sc, 19sc) At the end of rnd 12 fasten off and weave in ends.

BOOTEE TRIM

Rnd 1: With H hook and Expresso Bean, attach yarn to where you fastened off, 1sc in same st as joining, 1sc in each sc around. (17sc, 18sc, 24sc)

Rnd 2: 1sc in each sc around. Slst to end rnd. Fasten off and weave in ends. (17sc, 18sc, 24sc)

BUTTON BANDS – MAKE 4

Rnd 1: With H hook and Lake, ch 15, 1sc in second ch from hook, 1sc in next 12ch, 8sc in last ch. Now working on opposite side of ch, 1sc in next 13ch. Fasten off leaving a tail to sew with. Attach flaps to each side of bootee, making sure that the 8sc on the end of the flaps is on the outside of each bootee. Sew 2 button bands on each bootee. Sew buttons securely onto each end of flap.

Step 1: Working on opposite side of chain sole of bootee.

Step 2: Front post single crochet (fpsc).

Step 3: Working in loops behind fpsc.

Step 4: Tack ends of button bands to side of bootees.

Step 5: Sew buttons on opposite side of bands.

Legwarmers for Babies and Toddlers

Quick and easy to make with single crochets and shells.

Materials

- Premier Yarns/Deborah Norille Collection/Serenity Sock Weight/1.76oz/50g/230yds/210m #1 super fine weight 64% cotton/ 36% nylon
- 50%superwash Merino Wool, 25% Rayon made from bamboo, 25% Nylon
- Color number DN123–01 / Color name Pink Sugar / 2 skeins
- Yarn needle
- Scissors

- Hook: US D (3/3.25mm)

Gauge:
6sc rows – 1", 5sc –1"

Skill level: Easy

Glossary of abbreviations

bl– backloop
ch – chain
dc – double crochet
hdc – half double crochet
rnd(s) – round(s)
sc – single crochet
shell – 5dc in same st
sk – skip
slst – slip st

0–12 months size measures approximately 9" long x 6" circumference
18–24 months size measures approximately 11" long x 8" circumference
Recommendation: start each legwarmer with the same color so that your legwarmers look about the same.

LEGWARMER – MAKE 2
0–12 months size only
Ribbing Rows

Row 1: With D hook and Pink Sugar, ch5, 1sc in second ch from hook, 1sc in next 3ch. Turn. (4sc)

Rows 2–26: Ch1, 1sc in bl of next 4sc. Turn. (4sc) At end of row 26, hold row 1 up to row 26 and working thru both thicknesses, sc tog both ends to form cuff. Ch1 and turn cuff so that the seam is on the inside.

Rnd 1: Turn cuff on side and now working in ends of row, (1sc in next 4 ends of rows, 2sc in next end of row) rep 3 more times, 1sc in next 6 ends of rows. (30sc) Slst to join. Do not turn.

Rnds 2–6: Ch1, 1sc in same st as joining, 1sc in next 29sc. Slst to join. (30sc)

Rnd 7: Ch1, 1sc in same st as joining, sk next 2sc, shell in next sc, sk next 2sc, (1sc in next sc, sk next 2sc, shell in next sc, sk next 2sc) rep 3 more times. Slst to join. (5shells)

Rnd 8: Ch3, 4dc in same st as joining, sk next 2dc, 1sc in next dc, sk next 2dc, (shell in next sc, sk next 2dc, 1sc in next dc, sk next 2dc) rep 3 more time. Slst in top of ch3.

Rnd 9: Slst in next 2dc, ch1, 1sc in same dc, sk next 2dc, shell in next sc, sk next 2dc, (1sc in next dc, sk next 2dc, shell in next sc, sk next 2dc) rep 3 more times. Slst to first sc.

Rnd 10: Ch1, 1sc in same st as joining, 1sc in each dc and in each sc around. Slst to join. (30sc)

Rnds 11–15: Ch1, 1sc in same st as joining, 1sc in each sc around. Slst to join. (30sc)

Rnds 16–33: Repeat rnds 7–15 in sequence.

Rnds 34–36: Repeat rnds 7–9.

Rnd 37: Ch3, 1slst in next st, (ch3, 1slst in next st) rep around. Slst to join. Fasten off and weave in ends.

18–24 months size only

Row 1: With D hook and Pink Sugar, ch5, 1sc in second ch from hook, 1sc in next 3ch. Turn. (4sc)

Rows 2–30: Ch1, 1sc in bl of next 4sc. Turn. (4sc) At end of row 30, hold row

Step 1: 1sc in backloops.

Step 2: Sc both ends of cuff together.

1 up to row 30 and working thru both thicknesses, sc tog both ends to form cuff. Ch1 and turn cuff so that the seam is on the inside.

Rnd 1: Turn cuff on side and now working in ends of row, 1sc in each end of row. Slst to join. Do not turn. (30sc)

Rnd 2: Ch1, 1sc in same st as joining, 1sc in next 3sc, 2sc in next sc, (1sc in next 4sc, 2sc in next sc) rep around. Slst to join. (36sc)

Rnds 3–6: Ch1, 1sc in same st as joining, 1sc in next 35sc. Slst to join. (36sc)

Rnd 7: Ch1, 1sc in same st as joining, sk next 2sc, shell in next sc, sk next 2sc, (1sc in next sc, sk next 2sc, shell in next sc, sk next 2sc) rep 4 more times. Slst to join. (6 shells)

Rnd 8: Ch3, 4dc in same st as joining, sk next 2dc, 1sc in next dc, sk next 2dc, (shell in next sc, sk next 2dc, 1sc in next dc, sk next 2dc) rep 4 more times. Slst in top of ch3.

Rnd 9: Slst in next 2dc, ch1, 1sc in same dc, sk next 2dc, shell in next sc, sk next 2dc, (1sc in next dc, sk next 2dc, shell in next sc, sk next 2dc) rep 4 more times. Slst to first sc.

Rnd 10: Ch1, 1sc in same st as joining, 1sc in each dc and in each sc around. Slst to join. (36sc)

Rnds 11–15: Ch1, 1sc in same st as joining, 1sc in each sc around. Slst to join. (36sc)

Rnds 16–42: Repeat rnds 7–15 in sequence.

Rnds 43–45: Repeat rnds 7–9 once.

Rnd 46: Ch3, 1slst in next st, (ch3, 1slst in next st) rep around. Slst to join. Fasten off and weave in ends.

Step 3: Working in ends of rows.

Step 4: Working sc rnds then shell rnds.

Step 5: Shell rnds. Sc in middle of shell.

The finished legwarmer.

Acknowledgments

I would like to extend a huge thank-you to all of the parents who allowed us to photograph their beautiful children for this book; without them the book wouldn't be as special. I owe a particular thank-you to Tara who worked tirelessly — and with good humor! — to create the fantastic photographs that brought my designs to life.

Sandy Powers

Listed here are the yarn suppliers and retailers' Web sites that I used to obtain the gorgeous yarns used in this book:

A. C. Moore Arts & Crafts
www.acmoore.com

Jo-Ann Fabric and Craft Stores
www.joann.com

Sage Yarn & Notions
www.sageyarn.com

Cascade Yarns
www.cascadeyarns.com

Dale Norway
www.shopatron.com